Wash

1990

Margaret Thatcher

SPEECHES
TO THE
CONSERVATIVE
PARTY
CONFERENCE
1975–1988

Margaret Thatcher

SPEECHES TO THE CONSERVATIVE PARTY CONFERENCE 1975–1988

CONSERVATIVE POLITICAL CENTRE

This book was designed and produced by
Pardoe Blacker Limited, Lingfield, Surrey

ISBN 0 85070 793 5

Published by the Conservative Political Centre,
32 Smith Square, London SW1P 3HH.
Typeset by Southern Positives and Negatives
(SPAN), Lingfield, Surrey and printed by
Biddles Limited, Guildford, Surrey

First published April 1989

THE RIGHT HONOURABLE
MARGARET THATCHER
MP FRS
BECAME LEADER OF THE
CONSERVATIVE & UNIONIST
PARTY
IN FEBRUARY 1975
AND
PRIME MINISTER
IN MAY 1979.

THE PRODUCTION
OF THIS BOOK
HAS BEEN MADE
POSSIBLE BY
THE GENEROSITY
OF

Edited by
ALISTAIR B. COOKE
The Conservative Political Centre

CONTENTS

CONSERVATIVE
PARTY CONFERENCE

* BLACKPOOL *

10th October 1975

THE FIRST CONSERVATIVE PARTY CONFERENCE I ever attended was in 1946 and I came to it as an undergraduate representing Oxford University Conservative Association (I know our Cambridge supporters will not mind). That conference was held in this very hall and the platform then seemed a long way away and I had no thought of joining the lofty and distinguished people sitting up there, but our party is the party of equality of opportunity, as you can see.

I know you will understand the humility I feel at following in the footsteps of great men like our Leader in that year, Winston Churchill, a man called by destiny to raise the name of Britain to supreme heights in the history of the free world; in the footsteps of Anthony Eden, who set us the goal of a property-owning democracy – a goal we still pursue today; of Harold Macmillan whose leadership brought so many ambitions within the grasp of every citizen; of Alec Douglas-Home whose career of selfless public service earned the affection and admiration of us all; and of Edward Heath, who successfully led the Party to victory in 1970 and brilliantly led the nation into Europe in 1973.

During my lifetime all the leaders of the Conservative Party have served as Prime Minister and I hope the habit will continue. Our leaders have been different men with different qualities and different styles, but they all had one thing in common: each met the challenge of his time. Now, what is the challenge of our time? I believe there are two: to overcome the country's economic and financial problems, and to regain our confidence in Britain and ourselves.

The economic challenge has been debated at length this week in this hall. Last week it gave rise to the usual scenes of cordial brotherly strife. Day after day the comrades called one another far from comradely names and occasionally, when they remembered, they called us names too. Some of them, for example, suggested that I criticised Britain when I was overseas. They are wrong. It was not Britain I was criticising, it was Socialism, and I will go on criticising

Socialism and opposing Socialism because it is bad for Britain. Britain and Socialism are not the same thing, and as long as I have health and strength they never will be.

Whatever could I say about Britain that is half as damaging as what this Labour Government has done to our country? Let us look at the record. It is the Labour Government that has caused prices to rise at a record rate of 26 per cent a year. They told us the Social Contract would solve everything, but now everyone can see that the so-called contract was a fraud – a fraud for which the people of this country have had to pay a very high price. It is the Labour Government whose past policies are forcing unemployment higher than it need ever have been. Thousands more men and women are losing their jobs every day, and there are going to be men and women, many of them youngsters straight out of school, who will be without a job this winter because Socialist Ministers spent last year attacking us instead of attacking inflation.

It is the Labour Government that brought the level of production below that of the three-day week in 1974. We have really got a three-day week now, only it takes five days to do it. It is the Labour Government that has brought us record peace-time taxation. They have the usual Socialist disease: they have run out of other people's money. It is the Labour Government that has pushed public spending to record levels. How have they done it? By borrowing and borrowing. Never in the field of human credit has so much been owed.

Serious as the economic challenge is, the political and moral challenge is just as grave and perhaps even more so, because economic problems never start with economics. They have much deeper roots in human nature and roots in politics, and they do not finish at economics either. Labour's failure to cope, to look at the nation's problems from the viewpoint of the whole nation, and not just one section of it, has led to a loss of confidence, and to a sense of helplessness; and with it goes a feeling that Parliament, which ought to be in charge, is not in charge, and that the actions and decisions are taken elsewhere.

It goes even deeper than that, to the voices that seem anxious not to overcome our economic difficulties, but to exploit them, to destroy the free enterprise society and put a Marxist system in its place. Today those voices form a sizeable chorus in the parliamentary Labour Party, a chorus which, aided and abetted by the many constituency Labour Parties, seems to be growing in numbers. Mind you, any one who says this openly is promptly accused of seeing Reds Under the Beds, but look who is seeing them now. On his own admission, Mr Wilson has at last discovered that his own party is infiltrated by extreme Left Wingers, or to use his own words, it is infested with them. When even Mr Wilson gets scared about their success in capturing key positions in the Labour Party, should not the rest of us be? Should not the rest of us ask him, 'Where have you been while all this has been going on, and what are you doing about it?' The answer is nothing.

I sometimes think the Labour Party is like a pub where the mild is running out. If someone does not do something soon all that is left will be bitter, and all that is bitter will be Left.

Whenever I visit Communist countries their politicians never hesitate to boast about their achievements. They know them all by heart; they reel off the facts and figures, claiming this is the rich harvest of the Communist system. Yet they are not prosperous as we in the West are prosperous, and they are not free as we in the West are free.

Our capitalist system produces a far higher standard of prosperity and happiness because it believes in incentive and opportunity, and because it is founded on human dignity and freedom. Even the Russians have to go to a capitalist country – America – to buy enough wheat to feed their people – and that after more than 50 years of a State-controlled economy. Yet they boast incessantly, while we, who have so much more to boast about, forever criticise and decry. Is it not time we spoke up for our way of life? After all, no Western nation has to build a wall round itself to keep its people in.

So let us have no truck with those who say the free enterprise system has failed. What we face today is not a crisis of capitalism but of Socialism. No country can flourish if its economic and social life is dominated by nationalisation and State control.

The cause of our shortcomings does not, therefore, lie in private enterprise. Our problem is not that we have too little Socialism. It is that we have too much. If only the Labour Party in this country would act like Social Democrats in West Germany. If only they would stop trying to prove their Socialist virility by relentlessly nationalising one industry after another.

Of course, a halt to further State control will not on its own restore our belief in ourselves, because something else is happening to this country. We are witnessing a deliberate attack on our values, a deliberate attack on those who wish to promote merit and excellence, a deliberate attack on our heritage and our great past, and there are those who gnaw away at our national self-respect, rewriting British history as centuries of unrelieved gloom, oppression and failure – as days of hopelessness, not days of hope. And others, under the shelter of our education system, are ruthlessly attacking the minds of the young. Everyone who believes in freedom must be appalled at the tactics employed by the far Left in the systematic destruction of the North London Polytechnic – blatant tactics of intimidation designed to undermine the fundamental beliefs and values of every student, tactics pursued by people who are the first to insist on their own civil rights while seeking to deny them to the rest of us.

We must not be bullied or brainwashed out of our beliefs. No wonder so many of our people, some of the best and brightest, are depressed and talking of emigrating. Even so, I think they are wrong. They are giving up too soon. Many of the things we hold dear are threatened as never before, but none has yet been lost, so stay here, stay and help us defeat Socialism so that the Britain you have known may be the Britain your children will know.

These are the two great challenges of our time – the moral and political challenge, and the economic challenge. They have to be faced together and we have to master them both.

What are our chances of success? It depends on what kind of people we are. What kind of people are we? We are the people that in the past made Great Britain the workshop of the world, the people who persuaded others to buy British, not by begging them to do so but because it was best. We are a people who have received more Nobel Prizes than any other nation except America, and head for head we have done better than America, twice as well in fact.

We are the people who, among other things, invented the computer, the refrigerator, the electric motor, the stethoscope, rayon, the steam turbine, stainless steel, the tank, television, penicillin, radar, the jet engine, hovercraft, float glass and carbon fibres, etc. – oh, and the best half of Concorde.

We export more of what we produce than either West Germany, France, Japan or the United States, and well over 90 per cent of these exports come from private enterprise. It is a triumph for the private sector and all who work in it, and let us say so loud and clear.

With achievements like that who can doubt that Britain can have a great future, and what our friends abroad want to know is whether that future is going to happen.

Well, how can we Conservatives make it happen? Many of the details have already been dealt with in the conference debates. But policies and programmes should not just be a list of unrelated items. They are part of a total vision of the kind of life we want for our country and our children. Let me give you my vision: a man's right to work as he will, to spend what he earns, to own property, to have the State as servant and not as master – these are the British inheritance. They are the essence of a free country and on that freedom all our other freedoms depend.

But we want a free economy, not only because it guarantees our liberties, but also because it is the best way of creating wealth and prosperity for the whole country, and it is this prosperity alone which can give us the resources for better services for the community, better services for those in need.

By their attack on private enterprise, this Labour Government have made certain that there will be next to nothing available for improvements in our social services over the next few years. We must get private enterprise back on the road to recovery, not merely to give people more of their own money to spend as they choose, but to have more money to help the old and the sick and the handicapped. And the way to recovery is through profits, good profits today leading to high investment, leading to well-paid jobs, leading to a better standard of living tomorrow. No profits mean no investment and that means a dying industry geared to yesterday's world, and that means fewer jobs tomorrow. Other nations have recognised that for years now, and because they have recognised it they are going ahead faster than we are; and the gap between us will continue to increase unless we change our ways. The trouble here is that for years the Labour Party have made people feel that profits are guilty unless proved innocent.

When I visit factories and companies I do not find that those who actually work in them are against profits; on the contrary they want to work for a prosperous concern, a concern with a future – their future.

Governments must learn to leave these companies with enough of their own profits to produce the goods and jobs for tomorrow. If the Socialists will not or cannot, there will be no profit-making industry left to support the losses caused by fresh bouts of nationalisation. If anyone should murmur that I am preaching laissez-faire, let me say I am not arguing, and have never argued, that all we have to do is to let the economy run by itself. I believe that, just as each of us has an obligation to make the best of his talents, so governments have an obligation to create the framework within which we can do so – not only individual people, but individual firms and particularly small firms. If they concentrated on doing that, they would do a lot better than they are doing now. Some of the small firms will stay small but others will expand and become the great companies of the future. The Labour Government have pursued a disastrous vendetta against small businesses and the self-employed. We will reverse their damaging policies.

Nowhere is this more important than in agriculture, one of our most successful industries, made up almost entirely of small businesses. We live in a world in which food is no longer cheap or plentiful. Everything we cannot produce here must be imported at a high price. Yet the Government could not have destroyed the confidence of the industry more effectively if they had tried deliberately to do so with their formula of empty promises and penal taxation.

So today what is the picture? Depressed profits, low investment, no incentive, and, overshadowing everything, government spending, spending, spending far beyond the taxpayers' means.

To recover, to get from where we are to where we want to be – and I admit we would rather not be here – will take time. 'Economic policy', wrote Maynard Keynes, 'should not be a matter of tearing up by the roots but of slowly training a plant to grow in a different direction.'

It will take time to reduce public spending, to rebuild profits and incentives, and to benefit from the investments which must be made. But the sooner that time starts, the better it will be for Britain's unemployed and for Britain as a whole.

One of the reasons why this Labour Government have incurred more unemployment than any Conservative Government since the War is because they have concentrated too much on distributing what we have and too little on seeing that we have more.

We Conservatives hate unemployment. We hate the idea of men and women not being able to use their abilities. We deplore the waste of natural resources and the deep affront to people's dignity from being out of work through no fault of their own. It is ironic that we should be accused of wanting unemployment to solve our economic problems by the very Government which has produced a record post-war unemployment and is expecting more.

The record of Mr Wilson and his collegues on this is unparalleled in the history of political hypocrisy. We are now seeing the full consequences of nearly twenty months of Labour government. They have done the wrong things at the wrong time in the wrong way, and they have been a disaster for this country.

Now let me turn to something I spoke about in America. Some Socialists seem to believe that people should be numbers in a State computer. We believe they should be individuals. We are all unequal. No one, thank heavens, is quite like anyone else, however much the Socialists may pretend otherwise. We believe that everyone has the right to be unequal. But to us, every human being is equally important. Engineers, miners, manual workers, shop assistants, farm-workers, postmen, housewives – these are the essential foundations of our society, and without them there would be no nation. But there are others with special gifts who should also have their chance, because if the adventurers who strike out in new directions in science, tech-nology, medicine, commerce, and industry are hobbled, there can be no advance. The spirit of envy can destroy; it can never build. Every-one must be allowed to develop in the way he chooses the abilities he knows he has within him – and she knows she has within her.

Freedom to choose is something we take for granted until it is in danger of being taken away. Socialist governments set out perpetually to restrict the area of choice, and Conservative governments to increase it. We believe that you become a responsible citizen by making decisions for yourself, not by having them made for you. But they are made for you by Labour all right!

Take education: our education system used to serve us well. A child from an ordinary family, as I was, could use it as a ladder, as an advancement, but the Socialists, better at demolition than reconstruction, are destroying many good grammar schools. Now this is nothing to do with private education. It is opportunity and excellence in our State schools that are being diminished under Socialism. Naturally enough, parents do not like this, but in a Socialist society parents should be seen and not heard.

Another denial of choice is being applied to health. The private sector helps to keep some of our best doctors here, and so available part-time to the National Health Service. It also helps to bring in more money for the general health of the nation; but under Labour, private medicine is being squeezed out, and the result will be to add to the burden of the National Health Service without adding one penny to its income.

Let me make this absolutely clear: when we return to power we shall reverse Mrs Castle's stupid and spiteful attack on hospital pay beds. We Conservatives do not accept that because some people have no choice, no one should have it. Every family should have the right to spend their money, after tax, as they wish, and not as the Government dictates. Let us extend choice, extend the will to choose and the chance to choose.

I want to come now to the argument which Mr Wilson is trying to put across the country: namely, that the Labour Party is the natural party of government because it is the only one that the trade unions will accept. From what I saw on television last week, the Labour Party did not look like a party of government at all, let alone a natural one.

But let us examine the argument, because it is important. If we are told that a Conservative government could not govern because certain extreme leaders would not let it, then general elections are a mockery, we have arrived at the one-party State, and parliamentary democracy in this country will have perished. The democracy for which our fathers fought and died is not to be laid to rest as lightly as that.

When the next Conservative Government comes to power many trade unionists will have put it there. Millions of them vote for us at every election. I want to say this to them and to all of our supporters in industry: go out and join the work of your unions; go to their meetings and stay to the end, and learn the union rules as well as the far Left knows them. Remember that if parliamentary democracy dies free trade unions die with it.

I come last to what many would put first, the rule of law. The first people to uphold the law should be governments, and it is tragic that the Socialist Government, to its lasting shame, should have lost its nerve and shed its principles over the People's Republic of Clay Cross, and that a group of the Labour Party should have tried to turn the Shrewsbury pickets into martyrs. On both occasions the law was broken and on one violence was done. No decent society can live like that, and no responsible party should condone it. The first duty of government is to uphold the law, and if it tries to bob, weave and duck round that duty when it is inconvenient, the governed will do exactly the same thing, and then nothing will be safe, not home, not liberty, not life itself.

There is one part of this country where, tragically, defiance of the law is costing life day after day. In Northern Ireland our troops have the dangerous and thankless task of trying to keep the peace and hold a balance. We are proud of the way they have discharged their duty. This Party is pledged to support the unity of the United Kingdom, to preserve that unity and to protect the people, Catholic and Protestant alike. We believe our Armed Forces must remain until a genuine peace is made. Our thoughts are with them and our pride is with them, too.

I have spoken of the challenges which face us here in Britain – the challenge to recover economically and the challenge to recover our belief in ourselves – and I have shown our potential for recovery. I have dealt with some aspects of our strength and approach and I have tried to tell you something of my personal vision and my belief in the standards on which this nation was greatly built, on which it greatly thrived and from which in recent years it has greatly fallen away. I believe we are coming to yet another turning point in our long history. We can go on as we have been going and continue down, or we can stop and with a decisive act of will say 'Enough'.

Let all of us here today, and others far beyond this hall who believe in our cause, make that act of will. Let us proclaim our faith in a new and better future for our Party and our people; let us resolve to heal the wounds of a divided nation, and let that act of healing be the prelude to a lasting victory.

2

I WANT TO SPEAK to you today about the rebirth of a nation: our nation – the British nation.

It is customary at conferences to talk mainly about winning elections, to concentrate on the Party interest. There is nothing dishonourable about that. I am not against winning elections. On the contrary, I think that one of the problems facing this country is that our Party has not won enough of them lately – a situation we propose to remedy.

But for the Conservative Party politics has always been about something more than gaining power. It has been about serving the nation. We are above all a patriotic party, a national party; and so it is not we who have been obsessed this week with how to take party advantage of the present crisis. What's good for General Motors may be good for the USA. But nothing that's bad for Britain can ever be good for Conservatives. What we have been concerned with is how we can tackle this crisis, how we can ensure the prosperity, the freedom – yes – and the honour of Britain. The very survival of our laws, our institutions, our national character – that is what is at stake today.

Economically, Britain is on its knees. It is not unpatriotic to say this. It is no secret. It is known by people of all ages. By those old enough to remember the sacrifices of the war and who now ask what ever happened to the fruits of victory; by the young, born since the war, who have seen too much national failure; by those who leave this country in increasing numbers for other lands. For them, hope has withered and faith has gone sour. And for we who remain it is close to midnight. As Ted Heath said with such force on Wednesday, Britain is at the end of the road. As we all know, he is a man who never sold the truth to serve the hour. I am indeed grateful for what he said. Let us all have his courage.

The situation of our country grows daily, almost hourly, worse. As the bailiffs approach, can nothing be done? If the Labour Government is no longer able to act in the national interest, is there no alternative to the ruin of Britain? Yes, indeed there is – and that alternative is here at Brighton today.

But if we in the Conservative Party are to shoulder the responsibility of government, to chart a fresh course for our country, then we must first understand what has happened to us – where things have gone wrong – and why. I believe there are several reasons for what is known as 'the British sickness' – and they are not a criticism of the people of this country. They are a criticism of the Government of this country.

First, we have become the big spenders of Europe – spenders of other countries' money. The Labour Government of Harold Wilson and James Callaghan have spent and spent and spent again with unbridled extravagance. And they have exhausted the means to pay for it. They have nearly exhausted the patience and tolerance and respect of our friends. Under Labour the land of hope and glory has become the land of beg and borrow. Today, the Government are back once more at the money lenders for what may well be their last chance – and ours. For this time they are about to pledge the nation's credit to the hilt.

Secondly, increasing interference and direction of industry have stopped it doing its job properly. The Government have chopped and changed policies; they have created confusion and uncertainty. They have added countless burdens. They have destroyed profits. They have raised the cost of borrowing to intolerable heights. And they have demoralised management and they have sapped the will to work. No wonder investment in industry has slowed to a crawl.

The third reason – and it goes hand-in-glove with the second reason – is political rather than economic. It's the Labour Party's chronic schizophrenia about the future of free enterprise – although the world over, free enterprise has proved itself more efficient, and better able to produce a good standard of living than either Socialism or Communism; and although wherever free enterprise is strangled, freedom is strangled too. Even so, even against all that background, the Labour Party has remained confused and divided over whether free enterprise should be allowed to survive. Yet, in spite of everything, it has survived – so far. Not only that, but, taxed to the limit, it has been the prop and stay of the public sector. Today that survival is in danger. As everyone saw on their television screens last week, the Labour Party has now been taken over by extremists. After years of gnawing and burrowing away in the background, they have at last crept out of the woodwork – at of all places the Winter Gardens, Blackpool. It was a sight the country is unlikely ever to forget.

The Labour Party is now committed to a programme which is frankly and unashamedly Marxist, a programme initiated by its

National Executive and now firmly endorsed by its official Party Conference.

In the House of Commons the Labour Left may still be out-numbered, but their votes are vital to the continuance of Labour in office, and that gives them a strength out of proportion to their numbers. And make no mistake, that strength, those numbers, are growing. In the constituency Labour parties, in the Parliamentary Labour Party, in Transport House, in the Cabinet Room itself, the Marxists call an increasing number of tunes – in addition to 'The Red Flag'. With the Labour Party more bitterly divided than ever, let no one imagine that this country will be protected by Mr Callaghan's avuncular umbrella any more than it was protected by Sir Harold Wilson's raincoat. That umbrella was blown inside out at Blackpool.

Let's not mince words. The dividing line between the Labour Party programme and Communism is becoming harder and harder to detect. Indeed, in many respects Labour's programme is more extreme than those of many Communist parties of Western Europe. So I hope that anyone who votes Labour in future will be aware both of the people and the ideas they are in fact supporting. It is not surprising that after the events of last week Mr Callaghan should speak about a totalitarian threat. He should know all about that. He faces it in his own party. But it is arrogant and utterly wrong of him to suggest that the only alternative to his Government is dictatorship. He should have a higher opinion of the British people.

Ours is one of the oldest democracies in the world. Our citizens have a passion for liberty. They have fought for it, and died for it. Provided they know what is happening, they will never surrender to the extremists, whether of the Left or Right. We are made of sterner stuff than the Labour Party. The trouble about the Socialist leader is that he talks tough but he never acts tough – until it's too late. He talked tough last week. He condemned the pawn-shop philosophy of his supporters. He even spoke of the need to earn wealth before it's distributed. He even mentioned profits – and at a Labour conference!

Apart from reading our speeches, where have Mr Callaghan and his colleagues been for the last few years? After the energy crisis three years ago, who was attacking us for cutting public spending and tightening the money supply? Callaghan and Co. Who fought the October 1974 Election saying that inflation was under control? Who said that there would be no great rise in unemployment? Who claimed that the Social Contract would take care of all our troubles? Callaghan and Co. Who doubled public spending? Who doubled unemployment? Who saw prices go up by more than 50 pence in every pound? Callaghan and Co. Who said 'Steady as she goes' – and then steered straight for the rocks? You've guessed it. Callaghan and Co.

Now half the Cabinet are beginning to tell half the truth. So what are the chances they'll change course? Nil, I'm afraid. Because the very nature of the Labour Party prevents a Labour Government from doing what some of its members at long last realise must be done. For example, we are told that to cut public spending further is impossible because the Labour Party won't stand for it. What an appalling admission! If the country's economy is bleeding to death, the Labour Party must stand for it. We must all stand for it.

This brings us, not for the first time, to the question: 'Which comes first with the Labour leaders – party or country?' Don't tell me. It's too depressing. With their approach it's hardly surprising that Labour's record over the last two and a half years has been so disastrous. First, there was Harold Wilson's administration. There's no secret why he resigned. He took to the hills while the going was bad but before it got worse. Now we understand he's been found and brought back to the City. A plunging pound and Wilson found. There's no end to our troubles. And now we have Mr Callaghan. Between the pair of them, Sir Harold and Mr Callaghan and their wretched Governments have impoverished and all but bankrupted Britain. Socialism has failed our nation. Away with it, before it does the final damage.

Yesterday we heard that the Bank Rate had been raised to an unprecedented 15 per cent. You will remember in your time, Mr Chairman, 7 per cent was a crisis measure. Now 15 per cent. The Government are going on taking stop-gap measures to try to restore confidence in the £. They still won't or can't change course and take the painful steps that are needed.

What would be the attitude of the Conservative Party if the Government did at last lay the right measures before Parliament for its approval? That is an important question for us all. In our response to it, we must be careful not to fall into a trap; a trap in which the Government look to us to support them over difficult decisions, knowing full well they can then buy off their own Left wing by putting through further Socialist measures which the Left will demand.

It is no part of Conservative philosophy to help build a Socialist Britain. I have already said that the Conservative Party puts the national interest before short-term party advantage. But the national interest now requires not only that the Government should cut back their expenditure to reduce their borrowing, but also that they should drop the divisive legislation which they are steam-rolling through Parliament: Bills like the Dockwork Regulation Bill; like the national-isation of aircraft and shipbuilding; like the controversial Education and Health Bills. These Bills have nothing to do with saving the British economy. Indeed, they can only make that task much more difficult.

We must distinguish clearly between governments and the measures they introduce. A few good measures dictated by events cannot redeem the appalling record and intentions of this Labour administration. We do not oppose good measures, but we will fight ceaselessly against bad government. Because the Britain we are seeking is a Britain which could never be founded on Socialism.

The task of the next Conservative Government will be formidable. The sooner we start the better. We have two great obstacles to overcome – doubt and bewilderment. First, bewilderment about what should be done, because we seem to have tried every trick in the book. We have had National Plans and Pay Pauses, Price Freezes, Productivity Awards, Industrial Strategies and Growth Targets.

We have been promised that the next bright ploy will hit the bullseye: that blue skies are just around the corner; that we will soon turn the corner; that the light is about to appear at the end of the tunnel – I quote from Mr Callaghan's speeches in the past – that we are emerging from the valley of gloom; that we are heading for an economic miracle. We have had whole regiments of clichés marching into the sunset; but the problems just go on getting worse. So it's not surprising that people are bewildered. It's not surprising that they are uncertain. Uncertain whether the task of doing what needs to be done – whatever that may be – is possible for a government of any party. For the Labour Party. Or for the Conservative Party. They are cynical about politics and politicians. They fear that a free future cannot be saved. It can be saved.

We can overcome our doubts, we can rediscover our confidence; we can regain the respect of the rest of the world. The policies which are needed are dictated by common sense. That is the right approach. We have set out the broad lines in our strategy statement and we have shown how they stem from a clear, coherent political philosophy.

We have first to put our finances in order. We must live within our means. The Government must do so. And we must do so as a country. We can't go on like this. We are paying ourselves more than the value of what we produce. We are spending more than we earn. The gap has to be bridged. It can only be bridged at present by borrowing from overseas. But it cannot be bridged that way for ever. And at any moment, if we forfeit the confidence of those who lend to us, that bridge can collapse. It is crumbling now. The only way to safety is to stop borrowing and stop borrowing soon; and, moreover, to show that we can and will repay our debts in a strong currency and on time. That is usually the task of a Conservative government. To do that, the country must consume less than it produces. That means a drastic change in policies and in attitudes. But we shall have to proclaim openly that this is our purpose.

Once we have taken the immediate emergency measures which are needed, we must chart the course for years ahead. There, the country faces a choice. Who is to spend less? At one extreme the Treasury can try to make us, the people, economise by putting up taxes. At the other it can concentrate all its economies on the Government's own spending. There is not much doubt about the right decision. The Government is spending about £200 a year more than it is raising in taxes, for each man, woman and child in the country. Surely no one, (that is no one outside the National Executive Committee of the Labour Party), can believe in the long term that taxes should go up still more.

So the only common-sense answer is to reduce government spending. That is our answer. Economies started as a matter of urgency must be sustained deliberately, carefully and humanely over the period of a full Parliament. They won't be easy. They will not be popular, and we shall have to defer some of our hopes.

We have indicated in *The Right Approach* those areas where cuts must be made – by getting rid of Socialist programmes; by removing indiscriminate subsidies; by rooting out waste and extravagance; by applying cash limits; by economies in most major spending programmes other than defence, the police and those on which the needy must depend. That is a very similar strategy to that which the Australian Liberal Party, our counterparts, fought their election upon. They are now doing it. That shows it can be carried out in practice; and the people are supporting them because they knew the measures must be taken.

In opposition we cannot write our own public expenditure White Paper; it would be foolish to do so. But we may not be in opposition that much longer. So let me pledge that once we are the Government, what we have said we will do about public expenditure, we will do; and we will keep our word just as those other Conservative Governments that I have seen in action recently in Australia and New Zealand have kept theirs.

If the present Government have no stomach for the fight, let them depart.

Let us realise that their almost total commitment to extravagant government expenditure is not borne solely of compassion. Not a bit of it! It reflects a stubborn desire to regulate the day-to-day lives of rich and poor alike. The more a family has of its own money to spend, the more independent it is of the State. The more that is taken away from that family by taxation, the more that family are under the heel of the State; and that is where Socialism wants them.

The Socialists' battle cry is always the same; we hear it in Parliament. 'The Conservatives', they say 'want unemployment. Conservative cuts' they claim, 'would double or treble those out of work'. Now this is nonsense. And we must recognise it as nonsense. No party deliberately seeks the misery and waste of unemployment. But what is the history of the last two and a half years? It is a Labour government that has doubled the numbers out of work and set a shameful post-war record. And however well intentioned, it is Labour's policies that have brought this about.

Yet curiously enough they have neither the wit to acknowledge it nor the courage to change those policies. They doubled public spending. That led to a doubling of unemployment, because they bled productive industry white of the resources it needed to provide jobs. Today their policies threaten the ultimate disaster: an economic earthquake that would ruin the livelihood of thousands of families.

Of course we're not going to solve our problems just by cuts, just by restraint. Sometimes I think I have had enough of hearing of restraint. It was not restraint that brought us the achievements of Elizabethan England; it was not restraint that started the Industrial Revolution; it was not restraint that led Lord Nuffield to start building cars in a bicycle shop in Oxford. It wasn't restraint that inspired us to explore for oil in the North Sea and bring it ashore. It was incentive – positive, vital, driving, individual incentive. The incentive that was once the dynamo of this country but which today our youth are denied. Incentive that has been snuffed out by the Socialist State.

We Conservatives have to recreate the conditions cited by that wise French philosopher de Tocqueville – conditions which 'give men the courage to seek prosperity, the freedom to follow it up, the sense and habits to find it, and the assurance of reaping the benefits'. That says it all; everything that is not being done now but which we must do. We must break out of restraint if we are to have a prosperous and successful future. We shall do this by providing a stable economic background so that expansion and growth will pay and be seen to pay. We shall do it by letting profits rise to a level which offers a real incentive to expand. We shall do it by ensuring that men and women who invest their savings in their own business, or in someone else's business, can once more earn a reasonable return. We shall do it by following the example of other Conservative governments and cutting taxes as soon as we can. We shall encourage the production of wealth by spreading a share in its growth among those who have helped to create it.

That is the programme which will lead to expansion – picking up speed over the years. Expansion – leading to more jobs. Expansion – leading to higher wages. Expansion – leading eventually to more resources for the nation, so that we can have the same standards of social services as our more successful competitors enjoy. That is a realistic strategy, and it is one which offers hope to our nation.

These, then, are some of the guidelines of our strategy – prudent financial management and soundly based expansion. But there are many who will say: 'We agree, broadly, with what you want to do. But we are frightened that the trade unions won't let you do it'. This does less than justice both to us and the trade unions. One of the best debates that we have had here was on industrial relations. During that debate one speaker after another, Conservative trade unionists, Conservative negotiators and shop stewards, distinguished the role of trade unions from that of Parliament. What shone through was the difference between what we understand by a social contract and what the Socialists mean. If the phrase social contract means that the job of the trade union negotiator in a factory or office is to secure good pay for good work, to secure good terms and conditions of service, to secure extra rewards for extra skill and responsibility, then we support the Social Contract wholeheartedly.

We want to restore the right of unions and management to make the best bargain they can in circumstances they both know. So do most union leaders. But we believe that ideally there should first be a generally agreed basis for wage bargaining. This is a system which has worked elsewhere for years – in countries which have inflation rates far lower than ours. So, the first meaning of the Social Contract presents us with no problem. But Labour's social contract is not like that. It apparently allows a handful of trade union leaders to dictate to the Government the level of public spending, the number of industries to be nationalised, what the tax system should be, the terms on which we can borrow from the IMF – and so on and so on. I am bound to say to them: 'With great respect, that is not your job. It is Parliament's.' Parliament is the only body which represents all the people. The most famous definition of democracy is government of the people, by the people, for the people. Not government of a section of the people, by a section of the people, for a section of the people.

I agree with the speaker who said that if a trade union leader, or anyone else for that matter, wants to run the country, he or she should stand for Parliament. In the Conservative Party we would welcome some more of them as candidates, although I should warn them that selection committees are a law unto themselves, as many non-trade unionists have discovered. But those who believe in good jobs, in raising their standard of living by their own efforts, in working hard for themselves and their families – all of those people, whether they are trade union leaders or shop stewards or ordinary union members, whether they belong to a union or do not belong to any union at all – all of them should welcome the return of a Conservative government.

Let me make it absolutely clear that the next Conservative government will look forward to discussion and consultation with the trade union movement about the policies that are needed to save our country. As for confrontation, the confrontation that matters to us is confrontation with rising prices, with rising unemployment, with rising debts and with the grave threat to Britain's future. So nobody should allow the Labour Party to frighten them into thinking that there can be no domestic peace if we do what has to be done to save our economy. Common-sense policies must, and will, prevail if we fight hard enough.

And those who share our common-sense views are not a small, beleaguered minority. We are a party of ordinary people with ordinary hopes and beliefs, but with extraordinary qualities of tenacity and purpose. Not for nothing are we privileged to belong to probably the oldest and certainly the most successful democratic party over the world.

But in recent years we have had more than our share of disappointments at the polls. We have all too often won the argument, but lost in the ballot box. We have won minds – but we must now win hearts. This I believe we can do. Because today the Conservative Party is the truly national Party. On matters that concern ordinary men and women, it is we who represent the majority view, and the Socialists the minority. People are increasingly concerned about the quality of their children's education, but we are the Party that puts standards as our first priority. People want to buy rather than rent their homes. It is we, not the Socialists, who want to offer the opportunity of home ownership to everyone. People want protection from crime and vandalism in particular, and it is we who are the Party that will emphatically not economise on the police force.

People are becoming increasingly frustrated by the crushing weight of personal taxation in Britain, where we now have the highest starting rate of income tax in the world. We are the Party that wants to reduce taxation, while the Socialists never stop trying to raise it.

And we are the Party that believes it should pay more to work than to stay idle. A growing number of people are anxious about the strength of our armed forces. We are the Party that regards the defence of the realm as the overriding duty of any government. We want to see a defeat of terrorism, especially in Northern Ireland. But what a distortion, what a travesty of the truth it is for the Socialists to call themselves the party of working people. Today we are all working people. Today it is the Conservatives and not the Socialists who represent the true interests and hopes and aspirations of the working people. Above all else, let us get that message into every corner of the United Kingdom.

We are nearing the end of one of the best conferences we have had since the War. Speaker after speaker, from every walk of life, has come forward to join in debates that have not only been of high quality but have reflected the grave position in which our country finds itself.

Today I have tried to speak the truth to you as I see it – and through you to the nation – and beyond the nation to those who wait and watch from abroad, asking anxiously 'Where are the British going? What will they do?'

I call the Conservative Party now to a crusade. Not only the Conservative Party. I appeal to all those men and women of goodwill who do not want a Marxist future for themselves or their children or their children's children. This is not just a fight about national solvency. It is a fight about the very foundations of the social order. It is a crusade not merely to put a temporary brake on Socialism, but to stop its onward march once and for all. To do that we must reach out not only to the minds but to the hearts and feelings and to the deepest instincts of our people.

Let us be clear in our thinking. Let us be confident in our approach. but above all, let us be generous in our understanding. If, as has been said and I believe, the Conservative Party is the last bastion between Britain and disaster, then let that bastion be broad enough and large enough to accommodate all our people, Conservative and non-Conservative, trade unionists and non-trade unionists, those who have always been with us and those who have never been with us but who are prepared to support us now because they put country before party. Let no one be excluded from our crusade and let no one exclude himself. We are one nation. We may not know it with our brains but we know it with our roots.

I am deeply conscious of the challenge to our Party and of the responsibility I face as its Leader, but I believe we shall be sustained by millions who are hoping and praying today that we shall rise to the level of events. We must not fail them, and we will not fail them. As I look to our great history and then at our dismal present, I draw strength from the great and brave things this nation has achieved. I seem to see clearly, as a bright new day, the future that we can and must win back. As was said before another famous battle: 'It is true that we are in great danger; the greater therefore should our courage be'.

So let us be in good heart. We are not alone. Across the world, from Australia to Sweden, from New Zealand to West Germany, Socialism is on the way out. The tide is turning. Be in good heart and we will give this nation back a sense of pride and purpose. Be in good heart and we will give our people back their self-respect. Let nothing narrow or vindictive or self-righteous be any part of our crusade. Rather let us say with humility: 'We offer you hope and a new beginning. Together we shall meet the crisis of this country – and tomorrow the day will be ours'.

3

I WANT TO BEGIN with a confession. I do not greatly care for being in opposition, but we have certain plans to deal with that situation. I believe the essence of politics is not what you say, it is what you do, so I look to the day when we put Conservative principles into practice – in Government.

I look to the day when we throw off the Socialist yoke and turn together to the task of setting our country on the road to a real and lasting recovery. That day can be postponed but it cannot be put off for ever. One Thursday – it will be a day just like any other Thursday, and yet, I believe, it will be a day that will prove the turning point of our time – one Thursday the Labour Party will have to keep their appointment with the voters. It is a prospect I relish.

'Either back us or sack us,' says Mr Callaghan. Just give the people the chance, Jim, just give 'em the chance. He will not, of course, until he must. He dare not, which is why, instead of having a government with steel in its backbone we have got one with Steel in its pocket.

Last week at Brighton we were accused of 'an insatiable lust for power'. It is not the Tories who have wheeled and dealed and manoeuvred and manipulated to avoid one thing at all costs – facing the voters; it is Labour's limpet Government. Hence the Lib-Lab pact.

So much for Labour's political principle. So much for the Liberals' genuine conviction, and so much for the courage to stand by what you believe in, even if by standing by it you lose your seat. Better to lose your seat than your self-respect.

Just what is it that the Liberals have kept in office? A Government that for two and a half years overspent, over-taxed, interfered, nationalised, debased our currency and all but bankrupted Britain; in short, that acted like a Labour Government.

Mr Healey blandly refers to the horrors of 1974–5, but who was Chancellor of the Exchequer then? You have guessed – they were Healey's horrors. After him the deluge? No, *because* of him the deluge. 'The financial position has been reversed 180 degrees,' says the

Chancellor with a flourish. Quite so, because his policies have been reversed 180 degrees – by order of the IMF. Twelve months ago the four-budget-a-year man all but took the country over the cliff with him until, at the eleventh hour, he turned back from Heathrow in a panic and headed for home to take out the most massive mortgage in our history. The prescription the IMF forced his Government to swallow is the prescription we have long been advocating – a good sound sensible Conservative prescription. So my message to Moses is this: keep taking the tablets.

If Labour wants an election slogan I suggest – it is just a thought but one likes to be helpful – 'You *know* IMF government works.'

Some of the commentators are saying that the Prime Minister is stealing our clothes. Well, it is true that he has lost his own but he is going to look pretty ridiculous walking around in mine!

Of course, all of us are deeply thankful that the wealth of the North Sea has started to flow; but the North Sea is not a Socialist sea and its oil is not Socialist oil. It was found by private enterprise; it was drilled by private enterprise; and it is being brought ashore by private enterprise. So let us put the picture in perspective.

As the oil comes on stream, our balance of payments is going to look healthier. That is good news for Britain. Sterling should be safe from another Socialist slide. That is good news for Britain. The standard of living of our people might rise again, if only a little, after its catastrophic fall. That would be good news for Britain, too. As I have said before, good news for Britain is good news for the Conservative Party.

But look closer. The truth is that we are still grinding along in bottom gear, with our factories producing less than they were when Labour came to power. Real profits, and therefore investment, are still abysmally low; the number of men and women without a job is the highest since the War. And that is bad news for Britain.

Now take prices, if you can catch them! The Government boasts of its success in bringing down the rate of inflation. But even if it falls as far as Mr Healey predicts – and today not even his own No. 2 believes him – prices in Britain will still be going up faster than in other countries. If Labour survives into next year, prices will have doubled while they have been in power. Doubled! That is not an economic miracle. It is an economic and personal disaster.

At Brighton last week we saw Socialism wearing its pre-election face. Beware the leopard when it is quiet. It has not changed its spots; it just does not want its victim to know that it is there. Why was it so quiet last week at Brighton? Because it wants the people to believe that it is a gentle, well behaved, social democratic pussy-cat.

We all know the drill. In the run-up to each election the claws of Labour's extremists are not drawn; they are just *withdrawn*. The front men are paraded to talk quietly, moderately, almost sensibly. The Left-wing just allows them their little outing until the voters are once more in the trap.

Now suppose the election is over. Make a supreme effort and imagine that Labour has won, only for a moment. What then? The trap is sprung and Labour's extremists resume the drive towards a Britain modelled on Eastern Europe.

'It cannot happen here,' you say. But at Brighton the annual election to Labour's National Executive produced the same line-up as before; not a single Left-winger lost out. It is the same Executive which produced *Labour's Programme for Britain 1976*, and that programme remains official Labour Party policy 1977. Mr Benn was frank enough to say so, perhaps hoping the public was not listening.

Nationalise the banks and insurance companies. That is Labour policy. Do you like the idea of their hands on your savings? How do you fancy Mr Healey or Mr Benn as your friendly neighbourhood bank manager?

They want to nationalise all the land, not just some of it. All of it! They demand a free hand to take over almost any firm big or small, the building industry, the food industry, fishing, forestry, ports and many more. That is their policy, too. They want the power to make every business obey them. They want to cut tax relief for home buyers. They want higher income tax to pay for their plans. They want an immediate wealth tax on top of Capital Gains Tax, on top of Capital Transfer Tax. What is the point of building up your savings or your business if they are going to take it all away from you? But it's all there in their little red book. It's all official Labour Party policy. And to make it easier to ram through this frightening Socialist programme, they have just voted to abolish the House of Lords. There, behind the cosy Brighton front, you have the reality of Labour. Although, Mr President, I rather agree with you about the House of Lords. They will not find it easy to abolish it, because while half the Labour Party are trying to abolish it, the other half are trying to get in!

When the election comes, will this actually appear in their Manifesto? Some of it will, and if they were to win, sooner or later they will do it all. Because, whenever Labour win an election, the Tribune Group grow stronger and stronger and stronger. From one election to the next, Labour's programme gets meaner, more narrow, more Marxist. Britain, beware! The signpost reads: 'This way to the total Socialist State.' Destroying freedoms we have cherished and defended down the centuries doesn't worry the Far Left. They like everything about Eastern Europe – except, alas, going to live there – because, after all, the living standards there are very low for them.

So let no one say today there is no true difference between the parties, no real choice before the nation. That it not what the people think. Many men and women who had voted Labour all their lives turned to us in Ashfield, Stechford, Workington and Walsall. They know the Labour Party they used to vote for is not the Labour Party of today. The Party of Hugh Gaitskell has become a Party fit for Andy Bevan and Peter Hain. The disillusioned, the disenchanted, the courageous, the converted, we welcome them, one and all, to our cause. But the job of cleaning up Labour, the job of ditching the extremists, is not in our hands. It's in the hands of the people on that special Thursday for which we watch and wait and work.

If just five or six out of every 100 voters switch from Labour to Conservative at the election, they will slash the size of the Tribune Group by about a third, and on a swing of that size twenty-five Tribunites will lose their seats. And Britain will have a Conservative Government, a truly moderate Government, moderate not by order of our foreign creditors, but by genuine conviction, a Government in touch and in tune with the people, carrying out the sort of sensible, prudent policies that work so well in other countries.

Of course, that is not the picture our opponents are going to paint. And here let me make a personal prophecy. In the coming months you are going to see a carefully orchestrated campaign by the Labour Party and Labour Government to protray me as 'extremely this' or 'extremely that' – not to mention 'extremely the other'. A whole battery of extremist labels are going to be bandied about. Indeed, they are being bandied about already; and the closer the election looms, the faster and more furious will the bandying become. So just let me tell you a little about my 'extremism'.

I am *extremely* careful never to be extreme. I am *extremely* aware of the dangerous duplicity of Socialism, and *extremely* determined to turn back the tide before it destroys everything we hold dear. I am *extremely* disinclined to be deceived by the mask of moderation that Labour adopts whenever an Election is in the offing, a mask now being worn, as we saw last week, by all who would 'keep the red flag flying here'. Not if I can help it! The Conservative Party, now and always, flies the flag of one nation – and that flag is the Union Jack. So much for my so-called 'extremism'.

There is another word our opponents like. The word is 'reactionary.' They say that a Thatcher Government – and I must say that I like the sound of that; I like it a little more each time I hear it and they use it quite a lot so they must believe it – they say that a Thatcher Government would be reactionary. If to react against the politics of the last few years, which undermined our way of life and devastated our economy – if that is reactionary – then we are reactionary, and so are the vast majority of the British people.

They believe, as we do, that Government is far too big – indeed, the next generation were telling us so earlier in the week. They believe, as we do, that Government does not know all the answers, that it has downgraded the individual and upgraded the State.

We do not believe that if you cut back what Government does you diminish its authority. On the contrary, a government that did less, and therefore did it better, would strengthen its authority. Our approach was put very simply by a Chinese philosopher centuries ago: 'Govern a great nation,' he counselled, 'as you would cook a small fish. Don't overdo it.'

If you ask whether the next Conservative Government will cut controls and regulations and keep interference in people's lives to a minimum, my answer is 'Yes, that is exactly what we shall do.' The best reply to full-blooded Socialism is not milk and water Socialism, it is genuine Conservatism. For thirteen years from 1951 we curbed the powers of the State. Ask those who remember which they preferred: the steady increase in prosperity of the thirteen Tory years or the white-hot Socialist stagnation of Messrs Wilson and Callaghan?

By their fruits ye shall know them. What are the fruits of Socialism? Where is the prosperity? Where are the new jobs, the stable prices, the low taxes? Where is the money created by a thriving economy, to spend on our schools and our hospitals, on the pensioners, on the sick and the disabled?

Today we know Socialism by its broken promises; above all, by the broken promise of a fairer and more prosperous society. Socialism has not made society fairer, it has made it less fair. It has not made Britain richer, it has made it poorer. It has not distributed the rewards of achievement more widely, it has decimated them.

Just let us ask, and keep on asking, the question Labour can never answer: 'If your policies are right, why do they never work? And why is it only when you start doing some of the things we have told you to do that you ever take a few steps forward?'

But a few steps are not enough. If I have one message above all else it is this: I am not prepared to settle for the second, third or fourth best for Britain. I do not believe that our decline was inevitable any more than I believe that an accident of nature off our coasts has made our recovery automatic. I believe that if we confront – yes, 'confront' is the word I use – if we confront reality, if we pin our trust on the skill, the resource, and the courage of our people, then this country can work out its salvation and regain its prosperity, regain the respect of others and its own self-respect.

Some people regard this as dangerous talk. 'The Tories,' they say, 'want change; they want to challenge the rules and ideas and policies that govern Socialist society.' 'Risky,' they murmur. 'Right, of course, but risky – might upset Arthur Scargill or Jack Jones – better not do it, better not do it.' And there you have the root and heart of the choice facing our nation. What worries Jack Jones is that the leaders of his

Party are living too well. What worries us is that ordinary people are not living well enough.

That is why the next election will be so crucial. All elections are crucial, but this time the choice could be decisive for a generation, because this time how the country votes will settle which party is entrusted with the immense benefits of North Sea oil. If it is the Socialists, then the profits of free enterprise will be used to purchase Socialism, and to take more powers for the State. If it is the Conservatives, they will be used to give power back to the people. The choice is the classic choice. Labour will do what it has been doing for the last three years, only more so. We shall do what we have said we will do – set the people free.

The key question I am asked over and over again is: 'But will a Conservative Government be free? How will you get on with the trade unions, and will the trade unions allow a Conservative Government to govern?' Yes, the word is 'allow'. People who ask that question are already half way into Labour's trap. They have swallowed the bait and they are ripe for the catch. Here is the position: the Government dare not fight on their record or on any manifesto that would be acceptable both to their Marxist Left and to the people of Britain. So, like an unimaginative parrot, they keep on repeating: 'The Tories won't be able to work with the unions'. When the time comes, Jack Jones will be expected to mutter it; Hugh Scanlon to go along with it; and Clive Jenkins – he will almost certainly shout it. And it will not be true, unless the union leaders are determined to make it true.

Now let us take and face a hypothetical situation. Suppose they *are* so determined. Suppose they have already made up their minds to make the task of an elected Conservative Government impossible. Then we would face a situation in which an unelected minority was intent on getting rid of a government that it could not control and replacing it with one that it could. Is this what the union leaders seriously intend, to use their industrial muscle for political ends? I do not believe it. But people are asking: if it were so, what would happen? Could a handful of men with great power hold the nation to ransom? The answer is, it is possible. Should such a situation arise, for example in a vital nationalised industry, it would be presented as a conflict between Government and trade union. This would be false. The real conflict would be between union and people, because it would be the people who would suffer. It always is. In that case the duty of the Government, any Government, would be to act through Parliament on behalf of the nation as a whole. In a vital issue such as this, in which the Government had to take decisive action on a single specific matter, it would be important for the Government to know that it had the support of the majority of the people.

It is in that context, and that context only, that I have suggested a referendum to test public opinion. In those circumstances – in those special circumstances – I say: 'Let the people speak'. But I hope, and believe, the situation will never arise.

I would like to make two final points about the unions. First, a strong and responsible trade union movement is essential to this country, and its rights must be respected. Second, the belief that those rights take precedence over all other rights, and even over the law itself, could be fatal to this country. Happily, the great majority of trade unionists know this as well as, if not better than, some of their leaders. They know that while their leaders represent them at work, we represent them in Parliament.

We in the Conservative Party look forward to a long and fruitful association with the unions, because a Conservative Britain will be as much in the interests of union members as of the rest of the community. They know that taxes today are too high, that they torpedo talent, and that they must be cut; and that is what we Conservatives will do. We shall cut income tax, so that once again it is worth while to work harder and to learn a skill. We want to keep our best brains in Britain. We want to bring home some of those who have been driven abroad. We want to hold out to the enterprising businessman a reward which matches the risks of building up a firm. We want to renew the spark of incentive in our economy, because without that, new jobs cannot, and will not, be created. We want to leave everyone with more of his own money in his own pocket to spend as he pleases.

Our aim is to make tax collecting a declining industry. There are more civil servants in the Inland Revenue than there are sailors in the British Navy. If governments do not cut what *they* spend, we have to cut what *we* spend. There is one hand-out that the people really want today. That is the Government's hand out of their pocket.

This is the positive approach, and it is the key to getting industry going again. We do not believe that Government can run industry better than the people who work there. It cannot. Countries that are more successful than we are owe their economic achievements above all to free enterprise, and the benefits are not confined to a few of their citizens. They are spread among the many. The whole community benefits, because, 'when the tide comes in, all the boats rise'. Of course, no Government in a modern industrial society and certainly no sensible Conservative Government can wholly withdraw from the market place. But Government support for ailing industry will only produce an ailing economy unless it is selective, unless the circumstances are exceptional, and unless that support is directed to two overriding aims: moving the firm out of the red into the black and then back to independence as quickly as possible. A sure recipe for industrial blight is a Government that gives what amounts to a blanket guarantee that virtually any firm will be saved from the consequences of its own mistakes. No firm and no nation can behave indefinitely as though there is little difference between profit and loss, high production and low, success and failure.

In this as in so much else, Winston put his finger on it. 'It is a Socialist idea,' he said, 'that making profits is a vice. The real vice is making losses.'

We would like to see the workers who help to create the profits sharing them. The Labour Party want union leaders on boards of directors. We want more employees voting as shareholders at company meetings. Under a Conservative Government we hope that more of them will own a stake in industry and that more of them will own their own homes.

We Conservatives are a family party. We believe that in a healthy society more and more people should be able to buy the roof over their own heads. That is why we will give council tenants the right in law to buy their homes. That legislation, I promise you, will be announced in the first Queen's Speech of the next Conservative Government.

Let the Labour Party go on offering newly-weds a place on the waiting list for a house on a council estate which they can never call their own. We offer them a place that belongs to them, their own home in which to start life together and later to bring up their children.

What happens when the children go to school? We have got to stop destroying good schools in the name of equality. The main victims of Labour's recent attack on the direct grant schools have been able children from less well-off families. People from my sort of background needed grammar schools to compete with children from privileged homes like Shirley Williams and Anthony Wedgwood Benn.

Our aim in education is simple: it is to raise standards for all our children. That means fighting far more vigorously against that small minority which believes that the principal purpose of education is to instil contempt for democratic institutions. That is not education; it is political propaganda, and I see no reason why you and I and every other taxpayer should pay for it. These destroyers would also destroy respect for our laws and the order on which a civilised society is based.

People have asked me whether I am going to make the fight against crime an issue at the next election. No, I am not going to make it an issue. It is the people of Britain who are going to make it an issue. The old people in our city centres who are frightened to go out at night are going to make it an issue. The taxpayers and ratepayers who have to meet the bills for mindless vandalism – they are going to make it an issue. The parents, worried sick when their children go out on their own – they are going to make it an issue.

Yes, law and order will be an issue, and it will be a vital issue, at the election. If anyone thinks that is Right-wing, they should talk to the workers in the factories and the women at the supermarket.

The next Conservative Government will give more resources to the police. They are undermanned and poorly paid. We will bring them up to strength. We will give them the money to do the job. I do not intend to sit on the sidelines wringing my hands while London, Glasgow, Manchester, Birmingham and the rest of our cities go the way of New York.

But if the violence in Britain is deeply disturbing, it is nothing to what has been endured by the people of Northern Ireland for nearly ten years. What happens in Ulster touches us all; it is part of our country, our United Kingdom. So let the people of Ulster be assured of this: the Conservative Party stands rock firm for the Union of Great Britain and Northern Ireland.

Today I would like to express our deep and lasting admiration for Betty Williams and Mairead Corrigan, the Belfast Peace Women, who have been awarded the Nobel Peace Prize. Their courage symbolises to us and to the whole Western world the yearning of the people of Ulster for peace.

We honour with them the Royal Ulster Constabulary, the Ulster Defence Regiment, and our servicemen in Northern Ireland. I only wish that all the members of our armed forces who defend freedom there and in other parts of the world had a higher place in Socialist priorities. The Labour Party have cut present and future spending on defence by the staggering figure of £8½ billion. What sort of Government is it that so neglects the welfare of our servicemen? What sort of Government forces front-line soldiers into claiming rent rebates and makes many of them worse off than people who do not even try to work at all?

Our armed forces are poorly paid. They are denied the equipment, the stores, the back-up and the training that they know are vital to the job they do. Worse, they see the anti-Western wing of the Labour Party calling for still more gigantic cuts in defence, which a former Labour Defence Secretary said would mean, at best, neutrality and at worst, surrender. We have a Government that neglects our defences, a Government that lets down NATO so badly that our allies have rebuked it publicly. What a disgrace! A Government which spends money on nationalisation while cutting spending on the defence of the realm. As I promised President Carter last month, the next Conservative Government will see that our troops are properly paid, increase defence spending so that we can meet our obligations to our allies and, by strengthening the defence of the West, restore the morale of our fighting services.

Let us not forget – our first duty to freedom is to defend our own. It was to that end and purpose that I entered politics, and two years ago, in this hall, from this platform, I spoke to you for the first time as Leader of our Party. I remember well my nervousness, and pride, as I tried to tell you something of my personal vision and my hopes for our country and our people. I felt deeply my responsibility then. Today I feel it even more deeply. For much has happened between those two Octobers. Two years ago I spoke of a man's right to work as he will, to spend what he earns, to own property, to have the State as servant and not as master. And today the threat to those democratic values has doubled and redoubled.

I know only too well, as I go about the country, the fears felt for our British way of life. I know it from the letters I receive. And I know how many hopes ride with us today – the hopes of millions who are Conservative, and millions who are not, but who look to us because they feel instinctively that what is happening to their country threatens not only their freedom but everything that made it materially and morally great.

Paul Johnson expressed it movingly, and with a writer's clarity, the other day, when he resigned from the Labour Party. 'I have come to appreciate, perhaps for the first time in my life,' he wrote, 'the overwhelming strength of my attachment to the individual spirit. The paramount need to keep it alive, I now see, is so great as to override any other principle whatever.'

These are deeply anxious and disturbing days for those whose eyes are open and who value freedom, but provided we are alert and alive to the danger, then the human will of the growing and quietly determined majority must prevail. The responsibility that rests upon the Conservative Party is huge and humbling. But as autumn moves towards winter, and we brace ourselves for the great task that lies ahead, let us make this promise to the British people: We will discharge that task with all our strength and all our faith. We shall not fail our country.

4

CONSERVATIVE
PARTY CONFERENCE

* BRIGHTON *

13th October 1978

I MUST FIRST THANK YOU, Madam Chairman, for the wonderful heartwarming welcome. I confess that this is the biggest birthday party that I have ever had. I just do not know whether my parents had in mind the timing of the party conference, but if that is what is meant by family planning I am all for it.

One of the distinguished members of my shadow Cabinet sent me a birthday card today and said 'Don't think of it as another birthday; think of it as another year spent mastering the intricacies of a rewarding and demanding life'. That seemed to me a pretty fair description of the job.

Let us turn to the nation's business. Political life may be unpredictable. Dull it isn't. Last month the nation was privileged to watch on television the first broadcast ever to present a chronic case of cold feet as a noble act of patriotism. 'Let's see it through together,' said the Prime Minister in his now notorious announcement that there would be no election, 'in the national interest'.

Of course by seeing it through together he meant seeing it through with Labour. I am inclined to think that the people of this country will reject that invitation the moment that they are given the opportunity. Whenever the moment comes we are ready. As soon as Parliament reassembles we shall do all we can as a responsible Opposition to end the present damaging uncertainty, to defeat the Government and to bring about a general election.

But I must warn you that the dying days of this administration may well see one last wretched round of manipulation and manoeuvre, of private deals or public pacts or cosy little understandings – always, of course, 'in the national interest' – before the Government are finally dragged, kicking and screaming, to the polls. If that should be the case, so be it. I believe that the longer they wait the harder they will fall. But the harder, too, will be our task of halting and reversing the decline of Britain. Our party offers the nation nothing less than national revival, the deeply-needed, long-awaited and passionately longed-for recovery of our country. That recovery will depend on a decisive rejection of the Labour Party by the people and a renewed acceptance of our basic Conservative belief that the State is the servant, not the master of this nation.

But the problems we shall face are daunting. After nearly five years of Labour Government living standards have just got back to where they were when they took office. The Wilson-Callaghan years have left Britain close to the bottom of every international league table in terms of prices, in terms of jobs, and, above all, in terms of what we produce and what we owe to the rest of the world. Where they have left our country in terms of self-reliance and in terms of self-respect, in terms of national security I hardly have to tell you.

That is the legacy of Labour, and no amount of whistling in the dark by the Prime Minister or the Chancellor can change it. There is only one service they can do the nation now. It is to stand not upon the order of their going, but go. The damage that they have done to Britain is immeasurable. Our ancestors built a land of pride and hope and confidence in the future, a land whose influence grew out of all proportion to her size, whose constitution guaranteed a balance between freedom and order which used to be the British hallmark and became a model for the world. That was the heritage they handed down to us.

What would they think of Labour Britain today. A country in which people ask: 'Why work if you can get by without?'; 'Why save if your savings are taxed away, or inflated away or both?'; 'Why do a good job when you will probably make out just as well if you do a bad one?'; 'Why bother to get extra qualifications when differentials and earnings so often depend on political muscle, not personal merit?'

At home we are a country profoundly ill at ease with ourselves, while abroad a darkening and dangerous world scene confronts us. This is not just a Conservative analysis, it is a view shared here and overseas, not least by those who love this land and wish it well. In their franker moments even some Labour Ministers subscribe to it. 'Land of hope and glory, mother of the free' sounds as stirring and moving as ever, but it is less and less like the land we live in today. Why is that? What has happened to this country of ours that we thought we knew? It is not just a question of pinning down who is responsible, important though that is. The first step in clearing your mind about where to go is to understand how you got where you are.

Does what has happened to Britain over the last four and a half years imply that we have been governed by remarkably foolish people? No, though you may be able to think of one or two who would qualify under that heading. Is it the result of having been governed by unusually wicked people? No, there have been enough good intentions to pave the well-worn path twice over. The root of the matter is this: we have been ruled by men who live by illusions, the illusion that you can spend money you haven't earned without eventually going bankrupt or falling into the hands of your creditors; the illusion that real jobs can be conjured into existence by Government decree like rabbits out of a hat; the illusion that there is some other way of creating wealth than by hard work and satisfying your customers; the illusion that you can have freedom and enterprise without believing in free enterprise; the illusion that you can have an effective foreign policy without a strong defence force and a peaceful and orderly society without absolute respect for the law.

It is these and many other Labour fallacies that have brought Britain to where we are today. Of course it is true that things have not deteriorated quite so quickly since the crisis of 1976. It was then, you will remember, that Denis Healey was put on probation to the International Monetary Fund. A strange man, Mr Healey. He seems to think that being put on probation is some sort of achievement demanding recognition. Someone ought to tell him that you do not give the man who sets fire to your house a medal just because he phones for the fire brigade.

Last week at Blackpool he was boasting again about his success. He could see growing confidence throughout the economy. We are poised, he said, for another 'great leap forward'. But, he told the assembled comrades, there were two conditions which Labour had to fulfil to win the election. First, and I quote him again, 'we have got to keep inflation under control'. Agreed. 'And we have got to strengthen, not weaken the authority of Jim Callaghan in this movement and in this country.' Disagreed. 'Those,' said Mr Healey, 'are the things you have got to ponder before you cast your votes.' Well, the brothers pondered and then they voted. They voted overwhelmingly to throw overboard the Government's whole economic strategy, and with it, according to the Chancellor, the Prime Minister's authority.

The following day Mr Callaghan tried to restore it by speaking of the Government's 'inescapable responsibility' to deal with the present situation. He said nothing about his own inescapable responsibility for bringing that situation about. That is the charge against Mr Callaghan. Ask Sir Harold Wilson and Barbara Castle what they thought of his 'responsibility' nearly ten years ago when he fought tooth and nail against their plan for reforming the trade unions, for making them – yes – more responsible. 'In Place of Strife' they called it. The unions did not like it. Mr Callaghan saw it straight into the waste paper basket. The road to Blackpool 1978 was opened in 1969 by Mr Callaghan. He cut the tape and so long as it suited him he travelled steadily down the road he had himself opened without so much as a backward glance.

In 1974 during the dispute with the miners, how did he define responsibility then? I will tell you how. He went to Wales and said to the miners: 'I am here as Chairman of the British Labour Party because I wanted to come into the mining valleys to place the Labour Party firmly behind the miners' claim for a just and honest wage.' What would he say, what would the people of this country say, if the Chairman of our party had gone down to East London and announced: 'I am here as Chairman of the British Conservative Party because I wanted to come to Dagenham to place the Conservative Party firmly behind the Ford workers' claim for a just and honest wage'?

Well, now that the boot is on the other foot, what will the Conservatives do to him? Let me put his mind at rest. We are not going to follow in his footsteps. We won't accuse him of union bashing. We won't support a strike in breach of an agreement. We won't act irresponsibly, and he knows it. Nor do we rejoice at his discomfiture, for his problems are the country's problems. But a man who whets the tiger's appetite cannot expect sympathy when it turns and bites him.

Today the nation has a Prime Minister whose party has disowned his principal policy and destroyed the chief plank in his election strategy. Until last week that strategy was simple. Labour would play its union card, the one called 'special relationship'. The idea was this. A group of union leaders would try to persuade the country that if they were not allowed to call the tune there would be no music. Mind you, no union leader ever said: 'I shall overturn a Conservative Government'. It was always the union next door that was going to do that. For Labour this device would have had one splendid virtue. It would have made it possible for every Labour candidate to say in effect: 'Suppose Labour has created more unemployment than any Government since 1945; suppose it has produced a stagnant economy; suppose it has doubled prices; suppose it has nothing to offer but more and more nationalisation, more and more State control. The fact remains that only it can keep the unions happy and without this the economy will grind to a halt'.

That in a nutshell, was to be the Labour case when the election came. But the election did not come. Blackpool came – and with it, the great illumination.

Today, Labour's policies are at a dead end, economically and politically. This is not something to crow about. We do not hope for a country in ruins so that we can take over. We want to be elected so that we can do better, not because we could not possibly do worse.

The country is looking for a sign that we can succeed where Socialism has failed. Labour's dead end has to be our beginning. The idea that only Labour can talk to labour drowned in the sea at Blackpool. Let me now at our Conservative conference start the Conservative dialogue.

Here are the facts as I see them – and I am talking now straight to the union leaders:

'We Conservatives don't have a blueprint for instant success. There isn't one. But at least we start with this advantage. We know what not to do. That path has been clearly signposted.

'If a government takes too much in tax, everyone wants higher wages. If a government bails out those who bargain irresponsibly, where does the money come from? The pockets of those who bargain responsibly. If a government tries to level everyone down, with year after year of totally rigid incomes policies, it destroys incentive. If a government enforces those policies with the underworld sanctions of blackmail and blacklist, it undermines its own authority and Parliament's.

'For years the British disease has been the 'us' and 'them' philosophy. Many in industry are still infected with this virus. They still treat the factory not as a workplace but as a battlefield. When that happens the idea of a common interest between employers and employed flies out of the window and so does the truth that if your company prospers, you will too.

'Now, you the trade union leaders have great power. You can use it well or you can use it badly. But look at the position of your members today, and compare it with the position of workers in other free countries. Can you really say, can anyone really say, you have used your power well? You want higher wages, better pensions, shorter hours, more government spending, more investment, more – more – more – more.

'But where is this 'more' to come from? There is no more. There can be but there won't be unless we all produce it. You can no more separate pay from output than you can separate two blades of a pair of scissors and still have a sharp cutting edge.

'And here let me say plainly to the trade union leaders, you are often your own worst enemies. Why isn't there more? Because too often restrictive practices rob you of the one thing you have to sell – your productivity. Restrictive practices are encrusted like barnacles on our industrial life. They've been there for almost a century. They were designed to protect you from being exploited, but they have become the chief obstacle to your prosperity. How can it be otherwise? When two men insist on doing the work of one, there is only half as much for each.

'I understand your fears. You're afraid that producing more goods with fewer people will mean fewer jobs, and those fears are naturally stronger at a time of high unemployment. But you're wrong. The right way to attack unemployment is to produce more goods more cheaply and then more people can afford to buy them. Japan and Germany, mentioned several times this week – and rightly so – are doing precisely that and have been for years. Both have a large and growing share of our markets. Both are winning your customers and taking your jobs.

'Of course, we in Britain see the German success and want it here – the same living standards, the same output, the same low rate of inflation. But remember, what they have also had in Germany is strict control of the money supply, no rigid incomes policy, less state control than we have, lower personal tax and unions which are on the side of the future, not refighting the battles of the past.

'We shall do all that a government can to rebuild a free and prosperous Britain. We believe in realistic, responsible collective bargaining, free from government interference. Labour doesn't.

'We believe in encouraging competition, free enterprise, and profits in firms large and small. Labour doesn't.

'We believe in making substantial cuts in the tax on your pay packet. Labour doesn't. We will create conditions in which the value of the money you earn and the money you save can be protected.

'We will do these things. That I promise you. We'll play our part, if you, the trade union leaders, play yours, responsibly.

'Responsibility can't be defined by the Government setting a fixed percentage for everyone, because the circumstances are different in every concern in the country, whether nationalised or free. It's up to you, the trade union leaders, to act realistically in the light of all the facts, as the government must do. If you demand too much you will bargain your firm into bankruptcy and your members on to the dole. And no one wants that.

'Our approach works in other countries which are doing far better than we are. It worked here during thirteen years of Conservative government. You did better, Britain did better – infinitely better than today under Labour.

'Let's make it work again.'

That is our message to the unions. You can hear the same message in country after country. You can hear distant echoes of it even from Labour Ministers. It would be nice to think that this was due to an irreversible shift in the distribution of common sense. But it's really due to the nearness of an election and a swelling tide of protest from every taxpayer, every home owner, every parent in the land. I look forward to Labour's continuing conversion to good sense, and after the election, to their becoming a helpful Opposition in the new House of Commons.

So far I have spoken mainly of the practical and material failure of the last four Labour years and how we shall start to put things right. Let me turn now to something deeply damaging to this country.

Many of us remember the Labour Party as it used to be. In the old days it was at least a party of ideals. You didn't have to agree with

Labour to understand its appeal and respect its concern for the underdog. Gradually over the years there has been a change. I have no doubt that those ideals, those principles, are still alive today in the hearts of traditional Labour supporters. But among those who lead the Labour movement something has gone seriously wrong.

Just compare the years of Clement Attlee and Hugh Gaitskell with those of Harold Wilson and James Callaghan. Today, instead of the voice of compassion, the croak of the quango is heard in the land. There may not be enough jobs for the workers, but there are certainly plenty of jobs for the boys. That is the house that Harold built, to which his successor has not been slow to add a wing or two of his own.

Many in the Labour Party wonder what has happened to it. Socialism has gone sour. Today Labour seems to stand too often for expediency, for greed, for privilege, for policies that set one half of society against the other.

There are many reasons for this. One stems from that least attractive of emotions, envy. This spirit of envy is aimed not only at those privileged by birth and inherited wealth, like Mr Wedgwood Benn. It is also directed against those who have got on by ability and effort.

It is seen in Labour's bias against men and women who seek to better themselves and their families. Ordinary people – small business-men, the self-employed – are not to be allowed to rise on their own. They must rise collectively or not at all.

Object to merit and distinction and you're setting your face against quality, independence, originality, genius, against all the richness and variety of life. You are pinning down the swift and the sure and the strong, as Gulliver was pinned down by the little people of Lilliput.

A society like that cannot advance. Our civilisation has been built by generation after generation of men and women inspired by the will to excel. Without them we should still be living in the Stone Age. Without the strong who would provide for the weak? When you hold back the successful, you penalise those who need help.

Envy is dangerous, destructive, divisive – and revealing. It exposes the falsity of Labour's great claim that they're the party of care and compassion. It is the worst possible emotion to inspire a political party supposedly dedicated to improving the lot of ordinary working people. From there it is but a short step to the doctrine of class warfare. The Marxists in the Labour Party preach that this is not only just but necessary and inevitable.

But let me put this thought to you. If it is wrong to preach race hatred – and it is – why is it right to preach class hatred? If it is a crime to incite the public against a man simply because of the colour of his skin – and it is – why is it virtuous to do so just because of his position?

The political organisation of hatred is wrong – always and

everywhere. Class warfare is immoral, a poisonous relic of the past. Conservatives are as fallible, as human and therefore as given to making mistakes as the next man. But we don't preach hatred and we are not a party of envy.

Those who claim that we are a class party are standing the truth on its head. So, too, are those who claim that we are racists. Our determination to deal with the very real and difficult problems of immigration control has inspired Labour to a shameful attempt to frighten the coloured population of Britain.

Last month the Liberal leader added his voice to the chorus. No doubt in an effort to distract attention from his many deep and pressing problems, he too did his best – or worst – to pin the label of 'racialism' on the Conservative Party.

I realise that a drowning man will clutch at any straw. But let me remind young Mr Steel, millions of Conservatives were among those who spent five years of their lives fighting a war against racialism when he was still in short trousers.

It is true that Conservatives are going to cut the number of new immigrants coming into this country, and cut it substantially, because racial harmony is inseparable from control of the numbers coming in.

But let me say a word to those who are permanently and legally settled here, who have made their homes with us. Your responsibilities are the same as those of every other British citizen, and your opportunities ought to be. Compulsory repatriation is not, and never will be, our policy and anyone who tells you differently is deliberately misrepresenting us for his own ends.

Many other smears and charges will be thrown at us as election day comes nearer. But let us not be too concerned, however large the lie or absurd the charge. They are a sign of our opponents' desperation. For instance, you may have noticed, and so, I suspect, has the public, how often these charges contradict one another. One moment it is said that we have no policy, the next that our policies would bring about every disaster known to man. One moment Shadow Ministers are said to be notorious villains – well, here the 'villains' are. The next minute they are said to be unknown. Unknown? There's a charge from a party with household names like – let me see, now – Stanley Orme, not to mention Albert Booth. But then, no one does, do they?

Well, Mr Prime Minister, if there are any unknowns in the Shadow Cabinet we are all looking forward to becoming a lot better known at your earliest convenience.

Until then, national uncertainty continues, and with it the continued weakening of one of our most ancient and deep-rooted traditions – respect for, and safety under, the law. When a rule of law breaks down, fear takes over. There is no security in the streets, families feel unsafe even in their own homes, children are at risk, criminals prosper, men of violence flourish, the nightmare world of *A Clockwork Orange* becomes a reality.

Here in Britain in the last few years that world has become visibly nearer. We have seen some of the symptoms of the breakdown of the rule of law – the growth in the number of unsolved and unpunished crimes, especially violent crimes, overcrowded courts, an underpaid and undermanned police force, judges insulted by a senior Minister of the Crown. Sometimes, members of the Labour Party give the impression that as between the law and the law-breakers they are at best neutral.

We Conservatives are not neutral. We believe that to keep society free the law must be upheld. We are 100 per cent behind the police, the courts, the judges, and not least the law-abiding majority of citizens. To all those engaged in law enforcement we pledge not just our moral, but our practical, support. As for the law-breakers, whether they are professional criminals carrying firearms or political terrorists, or young thugs attacking the elderly, or those who think they can assault policemen with impunity, we say this: 'You will find in the new Conservative Government a remorseless and implacable opponent'.

The Conservative Party also stands for the defence of our realm. I am often told that there are no votes to be won by talking about defence and foreign policy. Well, I intend to go on talking about them, especially with elections to the European Parliament approaching. And, unlike Labour, we shall work to make a success of our place in the Community, and we shall not need to be prompted to honour our obligations to our NATO allies.

It was nearly three years ago that I warned of the growing danger of Soviet expansion. I was at once attacked by Labour's Defence Secretary and the Soviet leaders – stange company, you might think, for a British Cabinet Minister. What has happened since I made that speech?

The Soviet Union, through its Cuban mercenaries, has completed its Marxist takeover of Angola; Ethiopia has been turned into a Communist bastion in the Horn of Africa; there are now perhaps 40,000 Cubans in that continent, a deadly threat to the whole of Southern Africa. And as the Soviet threat becomes stronger, so the Labour Government has made Britain weaker. It has cut our forces time and again. We now have only 74 fighter planes to defend our country. We lost twice as many as that during one week of the Battle of Britain.

I am well aware that modern Phantoms have many times the firepower of the Spitfire or Hurricanes, but how does that help if you run out of Phantoms? There is a minimum level below which our defences cannot safely be allowed to fall. They have fallen below that level. And I give you this pledge: to bring them back to that minimum level will be the first charge on our national resources under the Conservative Government. It will not be easy, but there are no short cuts to security. There are only short cuts to defeat.

Conservatives too will see that our armed forces are properly paid. They do an indispensable job abroad and at home, not least in Northern Ireland.

I spent three memorable and moving days in Northern Ireland in June. The constancy and patience of the men and women of the Province who have endured so much pain through ten years of terror is something that I shall never forget. I know that there are those who say 'Leave them to solve their own problems and bring our boys back'. To them I must reply: 'If you wash your hands of Northern Ireland you wash them in blood'. So long as Ulster wishes to belong to the United Kingdom she will do so. That is the policy of the Conservative Party and it will be the policy of the next Conservative Government.

The next Conservative Government! I have spoken of what four years of Labour Government have done to Britain, materially and morally, at home and abroad. I hope that after this afternoon it will not be possible for anyone to say again that there is really not much difference between the parties. There is all the difference in the world and if it is the will of the country we will show the country and the world what that difference is.

May I end on a personal note? Long ago I learned two lessons of political life – to have faith and to take nothing for granted. When we meet again the election will be over. I would not take the result for granted, but I have faith that our time is coming and I pray that when it comes we use it well, for the task of restoring the unity and good name of our nation is immense.

I look back at the great figures who led our party in the past and after more than three years I still feel a little astonished that it has fallen to me to stand in their place. Now, as the test draws near, I ask your help, and not only yours – I ask it of all men and women who look to us today, who share with us our longing for a new beginning.

Of course, we in the Conservative Party want to win, but let us win for the right reason – not power for ourselves, but that this country of ours which we love so much, will find dignity and greatness and peace again.

Three years ago I said that we must heal the wounds of a divided nation. I say it again today with even greater urgency. There is a cause that brings us all together and binds us all together. We must learn again to be one nation or one day we shall be no nation. That is our Conservative faith. It is my personal faith and vision. As we move towards Government and service may it be our strength and inspiration. Then not only will victory be ours, but we shall be worthy of it.

5

CONSERVATIVE
PARTY CONFERENCE

---

* BLACKPOOL *

12th October 1979

ON THURSDAY, 3RD OF MAY, we won a great victory. Yes, it was a victory for realism and responsibility. It was also a victory for conviction and commitment – *your* conviction and *your* commitment. And it was a victory for loyalty and dedication – *your* loyalty, *your* dedication. Through the long years of Opposition you kept faith; and you will, I know, keep faith through the far longer years of Conservative Government that are to come.

An election victory such as ours is impossible without teamwork. It's invidious to single out this or that person for praise. However, one or two special tributes are due. We owe a tremendous debt to all our agents who did so magnificently. And I must also thank Lord Thorneycroft. He has been one of the most outstanding Chairmen the Conservative Party has ever had. This year he added another chapter to his memorable record of service to our Party and our country. Finally, I wish to say a personal thank you to someone who was and is always there to give strength and authority to our cause, not least in time of trouble. No leader of a Party can ever have been given more sound or more loyal advice that I have had from my friend and deputy, Willie Whitelaw.

The victory to which all of you in this hall gave so much was five years coming, but when it came it was handsome. We won with the largest swing since the war and the largest majority in votes. I was particularly pleased by the support we attracted: the largest trade union vote in our history; the young people, so many of whom saw no future under Labour and who turned to us; and all those who have voted Labour before and who, this time, voted Conservative.

Winning an election is a splendid thing, but it is only the prologue to the vital business of governing. The work that the new Conservative Government has begun is the most difficult, the most challenging that has faced any administration since the war. We have not wasted time. Already we have raised the pay of our police and armed forces. We have set in hand the sale of council houses and flats. In June we introduced our first Budget. We brought down income tax throughout the scale. We took care to protect the pensioners against inflation: next month's increases will be the largest in cash terms ever paid. And war widows' pensions have been relieved of tax altogether. At last they have received justice.

But all this is only the beginning. For this Government, it's not the first hundred days that count; it's the first five years – and the next five after that. We have to think in terms of several Parliaments. We have to move this country in a new direction – to change the way we look at things, to create a wholly new attitude of mind. Can it be done? Well, the people have taken the first step by electing us – some with passionate conviction; others, I don't doubt, more in hope than belief, their fingers tightly crossed. I understand their caution. So much has been promised in the past, so much has come to nothing, no wonder they are sceptical. And impatient. Already I can hear some of them saying: 'The Conservatives have been in five months. Things don't seem to be that much better. What's happening? Do you think the Conservatives can really do it?'

Yes, the Conservatives **can** do it. And we **will** do it. But it will take **time**. Time to tackle problems that have been neglected for years; time to change the approach to what Governments can do for people, and to what people should do for themselves; time to shake off the self-doubt induced by decades of dependence on the state as master, not as servant. It will take time – and it will not be easy.

The world has never offered us an easy living. There is no reason why it should. We have always had to go out and earn our living – the hard way. In the past we did not hesitate. We had great technical skill, quality, reliability. We built well, sold well. We delivered. The world bought British and British was best. Not German. Not Japanese. **British**. It was more than that. We knew that to keep ahead, we had to change. People looked to us as the front-runner for the future. Our success wasn't based on Government hand-outs, on protecting yesterday's jobs and fighting off tomorrow's. It wasn't based on envy or truculence or on endless battles between management and men, or between worker and fellow worker. We didn't become the workshop of the world by being the nation with the most strikes. I remember the words written on an old trade union banner: 'United to support, not combined to injure'. That is the way we were.

Today we still have great firms and industries. Today we still make much of value – but not enough. Industries that were once head and shoulders above their competitors have stumbled and fallen. It's said that we were exhausted by the war. Those who were utterly defeated can hardly have been less exhausted. Yet they have done infinitely better in the peace. It's said that Britain's time is up, that we have had our finest hour and the best we can look forward to is a future fit for Mr Benn to live in.

I don't accept these alibis. Of course we face great problems. Problems that have fed on each other year after year, becoming harder and harder to solve. We all know them. They go to the root of the hopes and fears of ordinary people: high inflation, high unemployment, high taxation, appalling industrial relations, the lowest productivity in the Western world. People have been led to believe that they had to choose between a capitalist wealth-creating society on the one hand and a caring compassionate society on the other.

But that is not the choice. The industrial countries that out-produce and out-sell us are precisely those countries with better social services and better pensions than we have. It is because they have strong wealth-creating industries that they have better benefits than we have. What our people seem to have lost is belief in the balance between production and welfare. This is the balance that we've got to find: to persuade our people that it's possible, through their own efforts, not only to halt our national decline, but to reverse it, requires new thinking, tenacity, and a willingness to look at things in a completely different way.

Is the nation ready to face reality? I believe it is. People are tired of false dawns and facile promises. If this country's story is to change, then we, the Conservatives, must rekindle the spirit which the Socialist years have all but extinguished.

Do we have the authority? Last month, I was accused of 'waving a phoney mandate'. In a democracy the word 'mandate' does not imply that a voter has read and accepted his Party's manifesto from end to end, and so not only knows, but is voting for, everything it contains. It would be absurd if it did. Not everyone who votes for a political party has read everything in its manifesto. Not everyone who votes for a political party has read anything in its manifesto. But when a voter makes his decision and slips his paper in the ballot box, he does know, broadly speaking, what the party of his choice stands for. In this age of mass communication he can hardly help knowing.

Those who voted Conservative know the principal policies we stood for, and that in voting for us they were voting for those policies. That was, and is, our mandate. We have every right to carry it out and we shall. Four economic issues were central to our Conservative campaign: inflation; public spending; income tax; and industrial relations.

Now these are not four separate and distinct issues. They are very closely related. You can't cut tax unless you curb public spending. For it is your tax which pays for public spending: The Government has no money of its own. Of course, if we had the money we could all think of good ways to spend it: hospitals which should have been modernised years ago, more help for the elderly, the sick, the disabled. But Government in one form or another already spends nearly half our entire national income. If Labour's lavish spending solved all problems we would have no problems left to solve. And inflation is a major problem which cannot be cured without curbing public spending. If the Government overspends, and borrows or prints money to meet the deficit, then prices and interest rates will go on rising – that's inflation – and the poor, and the pensioners, and the young home-buyers will all suffer.

But there are some who think they have a right to contract out of the effects of inflation, if they are organised in a powerful union with enough muscle to impose their will on a suffering public. What madness it is, that winter after winter we have the great set-piece battles, in which the powerful unions do so much damage to the industries on which their members' living standards depend; the struggles for wage increases disregard output, profit or any other measure of success. They ignore the reality that there is an inescapable link between prosperity and production. Since 1979 began, scarcely a week has passed without some group calling for higher pay. Listening to the chorus of pay demands, you might imagine that a one hundred per cent pay rise for everyone in the country would solve all our economic problems. But we all know that the only result would mean doubled prices. No one would have more food, more clothing, more anything.

The key to prosperity lies not in higher pay but in higher output. In 1979 you have all heard endless discussions about pay. How often have you heard similar discussions about how to raise output? The reason why Britain is today the third poorest nation in the European Community has little to do with pay but it has everything to do with production. We hanker after a West German standard of living. But we fail to recognise that you cannot have a West German standard of living with a British standard of output. The truth is very simple: West German pay plus British output per man equals inflation. And that is exactly what has been happening.

The unions win pay awards their members have not earned: the company pays out increases it can't afford: the prices to the customer go up: Government prints the money to make it all possible, and everyone congratulates it on its success as an honest broker, with or without beer and sandwiches at Number Ten. It has been happening for years. The result has been the most uncompetitive industry, the lowest economic growth rate and the highest rate of inflation in the industrialised world. And in the trade unions the lesson is drawn that militancy paid again, that the company did have the money. It didn't. The Government just printed its way out of trouble – until next time round.

This Government wants the greatest possible co-operation with both sides of industry and we will go a long way to get it. But we will not – repeat not – print money to finance excessive pay settlements.

Conquering inflation, controlling public spending and cutting taxes are the first three stages of a long journey. The fourth is to make certain limited, but essential, changes in the law on industrial relations. We have to make these changes in the law because, as we saw last winter, it is out of keeping with the needs of the time. When the trade union movement began, it set out to secure for its members a fair return for their work from employers. Today the conflict of interest is not so much between unions and employers as between unions and the nation, of which trade unionists and their families form a large part. It is the British people who have to bear the brunt of the suffering which strikes impose on society.

We have to bring about a fair and just balance between a man's right to withhold his labour and the determination of a small minority to impose its will upon the majority. As a Government we cannot, and will not, coerce people, but we can and we must protect people against coercion. And so, before the year is out, we shall introduce legislation concerning secret ballots, secondary picketing and the closed shop. The majority of the unions' own rank and file, so many of whom helped to elect this Government, welcomed our proposals. I hope that the union leaders, who have said that they will work with the elected Government of the day, will accept them too.

The days when only employers suffered from a strike are long since past. Today strikes affect trade union members and their families just like the rest of us. One union can deprive us all of coal, or food, or transport easily enough. What it cannot do is defend its members against similar action by other unions. If schools and hospital wards are closed, if there is no petrol at the pumps, no raw materials on the factory bench, the trade unions are as powerless as the rest of society, and when the bills come in for the stoppage they have to pay up too.

Recently there was a strike which prevented telephone bills from being sent out. The cost of that strike to the Post Office is £110 million. It will have to be paid for by everyone who uses the telephone. A £110 million loss caused by a strike of only 150 people in a public service. The recent two-days-a-week strike by the Engineering Union lost the industry £2,000 million sales. We may never make up these sales and we shall lose some of the jobs which depended on them. And who will send up a cheer? The Germans, the Japanese, the Swiss, the Americans. So instead of exporting engineering goods, we shall have exported engineering jobs.

I think the nation recognises – indeed has recognised for a long time – that trade union power is out of balance. That is why people are supporting us in legislating for trade union reform. We place special emphasis on the secret ballot. We believe that the great power wielded by unions calls for greater accountability to their members. And we are particularly concerned about the working of the closed shop. The closed shop, together with secondary picketing, makes it possible for small groups to close down whole industries with which they have no direct connection. Cross the picket line to do your job – and you risk losing both your union card **and** your job.

During the engineers' strike news reached London of a new resistance movement in East Anglia. Whole factories were actually working but so afraid were the employees of the consequences that they daren't reveal their identity, or that of the company, to the media. Millions of British workers go in fear of union power.

The demand for this Government to make changes is coming from the very people who experience this fear. It is coming from the trade unionists themselves. They want to escape from the rule of the militants. We heard it in the conference hall yesterday. They look to us to help them.

Today trade unions have more power over working people and their families than any boss has. Unions can only exist in a free society. Those who seek freedom for their own purposes should not deny that freedom to others.

I have been speaking of the deep and difficult problems of industry – most of it big industry. But the future of this country depends largely on the success of small businesses. I would like to read to you a letter which I have received from a small businessman in the West Midlands. I asked him whether I might read his letter and here it is:

'I thought I would write to you about the profound effect the change of Government has had upon one small businessman. In 1977, at the age of 38, I was so disillusioned with the Socialist regime and its policies that I could see no future for the small to medium business and sold my company to a large group and virtually retired.

Financially, this was a satisfactory state of affairs, but I yearned to get back into what I knew best. When your Government was elected, I hoped there would be a change of emphasis and indeed that is what has happened. The letter-head on which I write to you is of a new company which I have formed recently, and the biggest factor in its creation has been the steps which you have taken to restore incentive to work at all levels of the community. Not only can self-employed proprietors of small businesses keep more of the profits of those businesses but, more important, those good and productive employees who are patently worth a high level of wages are also feeling the benefit of more cash in the pocket and it is now worth their while to work that bit harder or longer as the case may be.'

He went on:

'Please stick to your policy. It is the only way that we shall eventually solve our problems. It may be hard to bear in the short term but I truly believe that the bulk of public opinion is now behind a return to the basic commonsense fact that the country as a whole cannot continue to be paid more and more money for less and less work.'

It is small businessmen like this who, given the chance will provide more jobs and more wealth, and the only Government from whom they will get the chance is this Conservative Government.

So far I have spoken of matters of vital concern to us here at home. But we have important responsibilities overseas as well, particularly Rhodesia. In his speech on Wednesday, Peter Carrington described the progress which has been made in our efforts to bring Rhodesia to independence with the widest possible international recognition. I understand and share your impatience to bring this about. There have been too many wasted opportunities.

It is Britain's responsibility, and Britain's alone, to bring Rhodesia to legal independence. But it is also in Rhodesia's interests that we should bring as many other countries as possible along with us in recognising an independent Rhodesia.

We undertook to give to Rhodesia the kind of independence constitution which we had given to our other former colonies. Those constitutions had certain fundamental principles in common. Each also contained provisions designed to meet the country's own particular circumstances. The same is true of the constitution under which we are ready to give independence to Rhodesia. Bishop Muzorewa has already accepted that constitution.

It must also be in Rhodesia's interests, and it is an inescapable duty for the British Government, to do everything possible to bring an end to a war which has caused the most cruel suffering. What is the purpose of continuing this war? It cannot be to bring about majority rule; that has already been accomplished. If it is to win power, then those who wish to do so must be prepared to proceed democratically through the ballot box and not through the bullet. At Lusaka the Heads of Government called for free and fair elections, supervised under the British Government's authority. We stand ready to do this.

I think we have some reason to be proud of what has been achieved since Lusaka. I trust that no one will now put that achievement in jeopardy. In view of what has been accomplished on the Independence Constitution the time for lifting sanctions cannot be far off. There is no longer any vestige of excuse for the conflict in Rhodesia to continue.

Nearer home in Europe we are part of a Community of some 250 million people. It's no use joining anything half-heartedly. Five months after taking office we have done much to restore the trust and confidence that the last Conservative Government enjoyed with our partners in Europe and the Labour Government did not. We are a committed member of the Community. But that does not mean that we are content with the way all its policies work.

If nothing is done, we are faced in 1980 with the appalling prospect of having to pay £1,000 million more to our European partners than we receive from them even though we have almost the lowest income per head in the Community. The hard pressed British taxpayer will not stand for paying still more in order to reduce the tax bills of our wealthier Community partners.

At the European Council in Strasbourg in June, we persuaded the other heads of government to agree to tackle this problem. We shall expect to make very real progress at the next European Council at the end of November. I do not underestimate the problems that face us on the Budget, in fisheries or in reforming the Common Agricultural Policy. But equally we must not underestimate our opportunities as members of the Community. The future of Western Europe is our future too.

What in the end are the objectives of the states which have come to make up the Community? The three most important are: international peace and justice; economic prosperity; freedom under the law.

We in Europe have unrivalled freedom. But we must never take it for granted. The dangers are greater now than they have ever been since 1945. The threat of the Soviet Union is ever present. It is growing continually. Their military spending goes up by five per cent a year. A Russian nuclear submarine is launched every six weeks. Every year the Russians turn out over 3,000 tanks and 1,500 combat aircraft. Their military research and development is enormous. The Soviet forces are organised and trained for attack. The Russians do not tell us why they are making this tremendous and costly effort to increase their military power. But we cannot ignore the fact that this power is there.

So far the North Atlantic Alliance has preserved our freedom. But in recent years the Soviet Union's growing strength has allowed them to pull ahead of the Alliance in many fields. We and our allies are resolved to make the effort that will restore the balance. We must keep up all our defences, whether nuclear or conventional. It is no good having first class nuclear forces if we can be overwhelmed by an enemy's conventional forces. Deterring aggression cannot be piecemeal. If it is, our effort is wasted.

Recently we and our allies have all become more and more alarmed at the number of modern Soviet nuclear weapons targeted on Western Europe. At the same time, NATO's own nuclear forces in Europe are out of date. We and our friends in NATO will soon have to decide whether to modernise our nuclear weapons. These will be difficult decisions for some of our allies, and we must expect to see the Soviet Union mount a powerful psychological campaign to prevent the Alliance from redressing the balance. We shall be looking very closely at President Brezhnev's recent speech to see whether it is the opening shot in that campaign or whether it is a genuine attempt to reduce tension in Europe.

Nor will we neglect our conventional forces. Our most precious asset is the men and women who serve in our Forces. We faced a grave situation on taking office. Recruitment was poor, and many of our most skilled and experienced servicemen were leaving the Forces. We immediately restored the pay of the Services to its proper level. We will keep it there. We have also taken steps to encourage the rebuilding of our Territorial Army and other reserve forces.

After so much neglect it will take time to put right the weaknesses. Nonetheless we must see that it is done. We owe it to our servicemen and women who give our country such magnificent service.

Nowhere has that service been more magnificent than in Northern Ireland. More than three hundred of our servicemen have given their lives there. Their bravery is matched by the courage of the Royal Ulster Constabulary and the Prison Service.

It is hard to speak of Northern Ireland without emotion. One thinks of Warrenpoint, of Lord Mountbatten, of Airey Neave. To any who seek to advance their cause by violence, and who claim to be soldiers of an army fighting for freedom, let me say in the words of the Lord Chancellor, Lord Hailsham: 'Such men are not soldiers. They are not an army. They are not fighting for freedom. They are fighting for chaos'.

We who believe in the one true freedom – freedom under the law – far outnumber and outweigh, in the strength of our resolve, those who set out to murder and to maim. No end could justify such means.

The British Government is doing everything possible to strengthen the security forces in the fight against the men of violence. Our goal is the same peace for which the Pope appealed so movingly during his visit to Ireland. To all the people of the Province of Ulster I repeat this pledge: we do not forget you, we will not abandon you. We must and we will find a way of restoring to you more control over your own affairs. We must and we will find a way to peace for your deeply troubled part of our United Kingdom.

We come to the closing moments of our victory Conference. It has been a Conference to remember. It was a victory to remember.

Throughout most of my life, the chief complaint made against politicians has been that they shrank from telling the truth when the truth was in the least unpleasant or controversial, that they were inclined to woo when it was their duty to warn, to please when it was their business to prophesy.

Early in my career, I decided that was one mistake I would not make. My harshest critics will perhaps agree that I have succeeded in that modest ambition; for the complaint they have against me is the opposite one – that I am inclined to speak my mind, even occasionally to nag!

Today, I have again pointed to the dangers as I see them and I have said what I believe the source of those dangers to be. But let us remember that we are a nation, and that a nation is an extended family. Families go through their hard times; they have to postpone cherished ambitions until they have the means to satisfy them. At times like these, the strength of the family is truly tested. It is then that the temptation is greatest for its members to start blaming one another and dissipating their strength in bitterness and bickering. Let us do all in our power to see one another's point of view, to widen the common ground on which we stand.

As we close our conference, a compassionate and united Party, I think of last week's events at Brighton. I think of those members of the Labour Party and trade unionists (including some leading ones) who see the movement **they** serve abandoning the ideals to which they have devoted their lives. They do not share our Conservative ideals – at least they think they don't – but they do want free and responsible trade unions to play an honourable part in the life of a free and responsible society. So do we.

I give them my pledge that my colleagues and I will continue to talk to them, to listen to their views, so long as it is understood that national policy is the sole responsibility of Government and Parliament. In return I would ask every man and woman who is called on in the next few months to take part in disruptive industrial action to consider the consequences for themselves, their children and their fellow countrymen. Our supreme loyalty is to the country and the things for which it stands.

Let us work together in hope and above all in friendship. On behalf of the Government to which you have given the task of leading this country out of the shadows let me close with these words: You gave us your trust. Be patient. We shall not betray that trust.

6

CONSERVATIVE
PARTY CONFERENCE

* BRIGHTON *

10th October 1980

MOST OF MY CABINET COLLEAGUES have started their speeches of reply by paying very well deserved tributes to their junior Ministers. At Number 10 I have no junior Ministers. There is just Dennis and me, and I could not do without him.

I am, however, very fortunate in having a marvellous deputy who is wonderful in all places, at all times, in all things – Willie Whitelaw.

At our party conference last year I said that the task in which the Government was engaged – to change the national attitude of mind – was the most challenging to face any British administration since the war. Challenge is exhilarating. This week we Conservatives have been taking stock, discussing the achievements, the set-backs and the work that lies ahead as we enter our second parliamentary year. As you said Mr Chairman, our debates have been stimulating and our debates have been constructive. This week has demonstrated that we are a party united in purpose, strategy and resolve. And we actually like one another.

When I am asked for a detailed forecast of what will happen in the coming months or years, I remember Sam Goldwyn's advice: 'Never prophesy, especially about the future'.

This week at Brighton we have heard a good deal about last week at Blackpool. I will have a little more to say about that strange assembly later, but for the moment I want to say just this. Because of what happened at that conference, there has been behind all our deliberations this week, a heightened awareness that now, more than ever, our Conservative Government must succeed. We just must, because now there is even more at stake than some had realised.

There are many things to be done to set this nation on the road to recovery, and I do not mean economic recovery alone, but a new independence of spirit and zest for achievement. It is sometimes said that because of our past we, as a people, expect too much and set our sights too high. That is not the way I see it. Rather is seems to me that throughout my life in politics our ambitions have steadily shrunk. Our response to disappointment has not been to lengthen our stride but to shorten the distance to be covered. But with confidence in ourselves and in our future what a nation we could be.

In its first seventeen months this Government have laid the foundations for recovery. We have undertaken a heavy load of legislation, a load we do not intend to repeat because we do not share the Socialist fantasy that achievement is measured by the number of laws you pass. But there was a formidable barricade of obstacles that we had to sweep aside. For a start, in his first Budget Geoffrey Howe began to restore incentives to stimulate the abilities and inventive genius of our people. Prosperity comes not from grand conferences of economists but by countless acts of personal self-confidence and self-reliance.

Under Geoffrey's stewardship, Britain has repaid $3,600 million of international debt, debt which had been run up by our predecessors. And we paid quite a lot of it before it was due. In the past twelve months Geoffrey has abolished exchange controls over which British Governments have dithered for decades. Our great enterprises are now free to seek opportunities overseas. This will help to secure our living standards long after North Sea oil has run out. This Government thinks about the future. We have made the first crucial changes in trade union law to remove the worst abuses of the closed shop, to restrict picketing to the place of work of the parties in dispute, and to encourage secret ballots. Jim Prior [Employment Secretary] has carried all these measures through with the support of the vast majority of trade union members. Keith Joseph, David Howell, John Nott and Norman Fowler [then Secretary of State for Industry, Energy, Trade and Transport respectively] have begun to break down the monopoly powers of nationalisation. Thanks to them, British Aerospace will soon be open to private investment. The monopoly of the Post Office and British Telecommunications is being diminished. The barriers to private generation of electricity for sale have been lifted. For the first time nationalised industries and public utilities can be investigated by the Monopolies Commission – a long overdue reform.

Free competition in road passenger transport promises travellers a better deal. Michael Heseltine [Environment Secretary] has given to millions – yes, millions – of council tenants the right to buy their own homes.

It was Anthony Eden who chose for us the goal of 'a property-owning democracy'. But for all the time that I have been in public affairs that has been beyond the reach of so many, who were denied the right to the most basic ownership of all – the homes in which they live. They wanted to buy. Many could afford to buy. But they happened to live under the jurisdiction of a Socialist council, which would not sell and did not believe in the independence that comes with ownership. Now Michael Heseltine has given them the chance to turn a dream into reality. And all this and a lot more in seventeen months.

The Left continues to refer with relish to the death of capitalism. Well, if this is the death of capitalism I must say that it is quite a way to go.

But all this will avail us little unless we achieve our prime economic objective – the defeat of inflation. Inflation destroys nations and societies as surely as invading armies do. Inflation is the parent of unemployment. It is the unseen robber of those who have saved. No policy which puts at risk the defeat of inflation – however great its short-term attraction – can be right. Our policy for the defeat of inflation is, in fact, traditional. It existed long before Sterling M3 embellished the Bank of England *Quarterly Bulletin*, or 'monetarism' became a convenient term of political invective.

But some people talk as if control of the money supply was a revolutionary policy. Yet it was an essential condition for the recovery of much of continental Europe. Those countries knew what was required for economic stability. Previously, they had lived through rampant inflation; they knew that it led to suitcase money, massive unemployment and the breakdown of society itself. They determined never to go that way again.

Today, after many years of monetary self-discipline, they have stable, prosperous economies better able than ours to withstand the buffeting of world recession. So at international conferences to discuss economic affairs many of my fellow Heads of Government find our policies not strange, unusual or revolutionary, but normal, sound and honest. And that is what they are. Their only question is: 'Has Britain the courage and resolve to sustain the discipline for long enough to break through to success?'

Yes, we have, and we shall. This Government are determined to stay with the policy and see it through to its conclusion. That is what marks this administration as one of the truly radical ministries of post-war Britain. Inflation is falling and should continue to fall.

Meanwhile we are not heedless of the hardships and worries that accompany the conquest of inflation. Foremost among these is unemployment. Today our country has more than two million unemployed. Now you can try to soften that figure in a dozen ways. You can point out – and it is quite legitimate to do so – that two million today does not mean what it meant in the 1930s; that the percentage of unemployment is much less now than it was then. You can add that today many more married women go out to work. You can stress that, because of the high birth-rate in the early 1960s, there is an unusually large number of school-leavers this year looking for work and that the same will be true for the next two years. You can emphasise that about a quarter of a million people find new jobs each month and therefore go off the unemployment register. And you can recall that there are nearly 25 million people in jobs compared with only about 18 million in the 1930s. You can point out that the Labour Party conveniently overlooks the fact that of the two million unemployed for which they blame us, nearly a million and a half were bequeathed by their Government.

But when all that has been said the fact remains that the level of unemployment in our country today is a human tragedy. Let me make it clear beyond doubt. I am profoundly concerned about unemployment. Human dignity and self-respect are undermined when men and women are condemned to idleness. The waste of a country's most precious assets – the talent and energy of its people – makes it the bounden duty of Government to seek a real and lasting cure.

If I could press a button and genuinely solve the unemployment problem, do you think that I would not press that button this instant? Does anyone imagine that there is the smallest political gain in letting this unemployment continue, or that there is some obscure economic religion which demands this unemployment as part of its ritual? This Government are pursuing the only policy which gives any hope of bringing our people back to real and lasting employment. It is no coincidence that those countries, of which I spoke earlier, which have had lower rates of inflation have also had lower levels of unemployment.

I know that there is another real worry affecting many of our people. Although they accept that our policies are right, they feel deeply that the burden of carrying them out is falling much more heavily on the private than on the public sector. They say that the public sector is enjoying advantages but the private sector is taking the knocks and at the same time maintaining those in the public sector with better pay and pensions than they enjoy.

I must tell you that I share this concern and understand the resentment. That is why I and my colleagues say that to add to public spending takes away the very money and resources that industry needs to stay in business, let alone to expand. Higher public spending, far from curing unemployment, can be the very vehicle that loses jobs and causes bankruptcies in trade and commerce. That is why we warned local authorities that since rates are frequently the biggest tax that industry now faces, increases in them can cripple local businesses. Councils must, therefore, learn to cut costs in the same way that companies have to.

That is why I stress that if those who work in public authorities take for themselves large pay increases they leave less to be spent on equipment and new buildings. That in turn deprives the private sector of the orders it needs, especially some of those industries in the hard pressed regions. Those in the public sector have a duty to those in the private sector not to take out so much in pay that they cause others unemployment. That is why we point out that every time high wage settlements in nationalised monopolies lead to higher charges for telephones, electricity, coal and water, they can drive companies out of business and cost other people their jobs.

If spending money like water was the answer to our country's problems, we would have no problems now. If ever a nation has spent, spent, spent and spent again, ours has. Today that dream is over. All of that money has got us nowhere but it still has to come from somewhere. Those who urge us to relax the squeeze, to spend yet more money indiscriminately in the belief that it will help the unemployed and the small businessman are not being kind or compassionate or caring. They are not the friends of the unemployed or the small business. They are asking us to do again the very thing that causes the problems in the first place. We have made this point repeatedly.

I am accused of lecturing or preaching about this. I suppose it is a critic's way of saying 'Well, we know it is true, but we have to carp at something'. I do not care about that. But I do care about the future of free enterprise, the jobs and exports it provides and the independence it brings to our people. Independence? Yes, but let us be clear what we mean by that. Independence does not mean contracting out of all relationships with others. A nation can be free but it will not stay free for long if it has no friends and no alliances. Above all, it will not stay free if it cannot pay its own way in the world. By the same token, an individual needs to be part of a community and to feel that he is part of it. There is more to this than the chance to earn a living for himself and his family, essential though that is.

Of course, our vision and our aims go far beyond the complex arguments of economics, but unless we get the economy right we shall deny our people the opportunity to share that vision and to see beyond the narrow horizons of economic necessity. Without a healthy economy, we cannot have a healthy society. Without a healthy society, the economy will not stay healthy for long.

But it is not the State that creates a healthy society. When the State grows too powerful people feel that they count for less and less. The State drains society, not only of its wealth but of initiative, of energy, the will to improve and innovate as well as to preserve what is best. Our aim is to let people feel that they count for more and more. If we cannot trust the deepest instincts of our people we should not be in politics at all. Some aspects of our present society really do offend those instincts.

Decent people do want to do a proper job at work, not to be restrained or intimidated from giving value for money. They believe that honesty should be respected, not derided. They see crime and violence as a threat not just to society but to their own orderly way of life. They want to be allowed to bring up their children in these beliefs, without the fear that their efforts will be daily frustrated in the name of progress or free expression. Indeed, that is what family life is all about.

There is not a generation gap in a happy and united family. People yearn to be able to rely on some generally accepted standards. Without them you have not got a society at all, you have purposeless anarchy. A healthy society is not created by its institutions, either. Great schools and universities do not make a great nation any more than great armies do. Only a great nation can create and involve great institutions – of learning, of healing, of scientific advance. And a great nation is the voluntary creation of its people – a people composed of men and women whose pride in themselves is founded on the knowledge of what they can give to a community of which they in turn can be proud.

If our people feel that they are part of a great nation and they are prepared to will the means to keep it great, a great nation we shall be, and shall remain. So, what can stop us from achieving this? What then stands in our way? The prospect of another winter of discontent? I suppose it might.

But I prefer to believe that certain lessons have been learnt from experience, that we are coming, slowly, painfully, to an autumn of understanding. And I hope that it will be followed by a winter of common sense. If it is not, we shall not be diverted from our course. To those waiting with bated breath for that favourite media catchphrase, the 'U-turn', I have only one thing to say. 'You turn if you want to. The lady's not for turning.' I say that not only to you but to our friends overseas and also to those who are not friends.

In foreign affairs we have pursued our national interest robustly while remaining alive to the needs and interests of others. We have acted where our predecessors dithered and here I pay tribute to Lord Carrington. When I think of our much-travelled Foreign Secretary I am reminded of the advert, you know the one I mean, about 'The peer that reaches those foreign parts that other peers cannot reach.'

Long before we came into office, and therefore long before the invasion of Afghanistan, I was pointing to the threat from the East. I was accused of scaremongering. But events have more than justified my words. Soviet marxism is ideologically, politically and morally bankrupt. But militarily the Soviet Union is a powerful and growing threat.

Yet it was Mr Kosygin who said 'No peace-loving country, no person of integrity, should remain indifferent when an aggressor holds human life and world opinion in insolent contempt.' We agree. The British Government are not indifferent to the occupation of Afghanistan. We shall not allow it to be forgotten. Unless and until the

Soviet troops are withdrawn other nations are bound to wonder which of them may be next. Of course there are those who say that by speaking out we are complicating East-West relations, that we are endangering detente. But the real danger would lie in keeping silent. Detente is indivisible and it is a two-way process.

The Soviet Union cannot conduct wars by proxy in South-East Asia and Africa, foment trouble in the Middle East and Caribbean and invade neighbouring countries and still expect to conduct business as usual. Unless detente is pursued by both sides it can be pursued by neither, and it is a delusion to suppose otherwise. That is the message we shall be delivering loud and clear at the meeting of the European Security Conference in Madrid in the weeks immediately ahead.

But we shall also be reminding the other parties in Madrid that the Helsinki Accord was supposed to promote the freer movement of people and ideas. The Soviet Government's response so far has been a campaign of repression worse than any since Stalin's day. It had been hoped that Helsinki would open gates across Europe. In fact, the guards today are better armed and the walls are no lower. But behind those walls the human spirit is unvanquished.

The workers of Poland in their millions have signalled their determination to participate in the shaping of their destiny. We salute them. Marxists claim that the capitalist system is in crisis. But the Polish workers have shown that it is the Communist system that is in crisis. The Polish people should be left to work out their own future without external interference.

At every party conference, and every November in Parliament, we used to face difficult decisions over Rhodesia and over sanctions. But no longer. Since we last met the success at Lancaster House, and thereafter in Salisbury – a success won in the face of all the odds – has created new respect for Britain. It has given fresh hope to those grappling with the terrible problems of Southern Africa. It has given the Commonwealth new strength and unity. Now it is for the new nation, Zimbabwe, to build her own future with the support of all those who believe that democracy has a place in Africa, and we wish her well.

We showed over Rhodesia that the hallmarks of Tory policy are, as they have always been, realism and resolve. Not for us the disastrous fantasies of unilateral disarmament, of withdrawal from NATO, of abandoning Northern Ireland.

The irresponsibility of the Left on defence increases as the dangers which we face loom larger. We for our part, under Francis Pym's brilliant leadership, have chosen a defence policy which potential foes will respect.

We are acquiring, with the co-operation of the United States Government, the Trident missile system. This will ensure the credibility of our strategic deterrent until the end of the century and beyond, and it was very important for the reputation of Britain abroad that we should keep our independent nuclear deterrent, as well as for our citizens here. We have agreed to the stationing of Cruise missiles in this country. The unilateralists object, but the recent willingness of the Soviet Government to open a new round of arms control negotiations shows the wisdom of our firmness.

We intend to maintain and, where possible, to improve our conventional forces so as to pull our weight in the Alliance. We have no wish to seek a free ride at the expense of our Allies. We will play our full part.

In Europe we have shown that it is possible to combine a vigorous defence of our own interests with a deep commitment to the idea and to the ideals of the Community. The last Government were well aware that Britain's budget contribution was grossly unfair. They failed to do anything about it. We negotiated a satisfactory arrangement which will give us and our partners time to tackle the underlying issues. We have resolved the difficulties of New Zealand's lamb trade with the Community in a way which protects the interests of the farmers in New Zealand while giving our own farmers and our own housewives an excellent deal, and Peter Walker [then Minister of Agriculture] deserves to be congratulated on his success. Now he is two-thirds on his way to success in making important progress towards agreement on a common fisheries policy. That is very important to our people. There are many, many people whose livelihoods depend on it.

We face many other problems in the Community, but I am confident that they too will yield to the firm, yet fair, approach which has already proved so much more effective that the previous Government's five years of procrastination.

With each day it becomes clearer that in the wider world we face darkening horizons, and the war between Iran and Iraq is the latest symptom of a deeper malady. Europe and North America are centres of stability in an increasingly anxious world. The Community and the Alliance are the guarantee to other countries that democracy and freedom of choice are still possible. They stand for order and the rule of law in an age when disorder and lawlessness are ever more widespread.

The British Government intend to stand by both these great institutions, the Community and NATO. We will not betray them.

The restoration of Britain's place in the world and of the West's confidence in its own destiny are two aspects of the same process. No doubt there will be unexpected twists in the road, but with wisdom and resolution we can reach our goal. I believe we will show the wisdom and you may be certain that we will show the resolution.

In his warm-hearted and generous speech, Peter Thorneycroft

[then Party Chairman] said that, when people are called upon to lead great nations they must look into the hearts and minds of the people whom they seek to govern. I would add that those who seek to govern must in turn be willing to allow their hearts and minds to lie open to the people.

This afternoon I have tried to set before you some of my most deeply held convictions and beliefs. This Party, which I am privileged to serve, and this Government, which I am proud to lead, are engaged in the massive task of restoring confidence and stability to our people.

I have always known that that task was vital. Since last week it has become even more vital than ever. We close our conference in the aftermath of that sinister Utopia unveiled at Blackpool. Let Labour's Orwellian nightmare of the Left be the spur for us to dedicate with a new urgency our every ounce of energy and moral strength to rebuild the fortunes of this free nation.

If we were to fail, that freedom could be imperilled. So let us resist the blandishments of the faint hearts; let us ignore the howls and threats of the extremists; let us stand together and do our duty, and we shall not fail.

7

CONSERVATIVE
PARTY CONFERENCE

* BLACKPOOL *

16th October 1981

SIX AND A HALF YEARS AGO I asked Peter Thorneycroft to become our Chairman. Of course I was anxious whether he would agree to take on the very heavy responsibilities that go with the Chairmanship. But my anxiety was misplaced. He who had already given more than forty years' service to our party wanted to do more. We all came to respect his wise judgement, his zeal for our cause, his breadth of vision and his devotion to the enduring honour of our country. It was typical of his magnanimity that he himself suggested that I should appoint a younger Chairman. I know that it is the wish of all us that we should send to Peter and Carla on the last day of our conference a message of affection and of gratitude for the unique qualities which he placed unreservedly at the service of the Party in which he believes so deeply.

And to our present Chairman may I say this: I want to let you into a secret. I asked Peter's advice about you. With that characteristic caution and understatement he said 'I think he'd do it rather well' – and so say all of us.

This week in Blackpool we have had the grand assize of the nation. Once more the Conservative Party has demonstrated that it is the party of all the people. We are not here to manipulate millions of block votes in some travesty of democracy; nor were we drawn here by the tinsel and glamour of a marriage of convenience. We are here as representatives of a myriad of different interests from every con-stituency in the land. We are here because we share a deep and abiding concern for the future of our country and our party.

There has been strenuous discussion and dissent. I welcome it. For years, as our conference has assembled, I have grown used to the charge that we are bland and anodyne, careful to avoid differences. I do not think that that is a charge that can be levelled at us this year.

We have witnessed here this week a party conscious of its awesome responsibilities as Government at an immensely difficult time, difficult not only for us but for many other countries in the world as well, for we are not alone in our problems. The diversity of our party is not a source of weakness; it is a part of our strength, for it is a reflection of the personal commitment that each one of us brings to the task that lies ahead. Let me say at once that I am glad that Ted Heath addressed our conference and delighted that he will be helping us in the Croydon by-election.

Our country is weathering stormy waters. We may have different ideas on how best to navigate but we sail the same ocean and in the same ship.

I have listened to much of the debate that has taken place in this hall and, you know, I seem to have heard a good deal of what has been said to us around and, even beyond, the fringe. This afternoon I want to draw together what seem to me to be the main strands of your wisdom and advice to the Government and to express some of your worries.

First among these is the deep and heartfelt concern for the personal hardship and waste reflected in every factory closure and redundancy. I learnt from childhood the dignity which comes from work and, by contrast, the affront to self-esteem which comes from enforced idleness. For us, work was the only way of life we knew, and we were brought up to believe that it was not only a necessity but a virtue.

The concern of this conference is focused on the plight of the unemployed. But we seek not only to display and demonstrate that concern but to find and pursue those policies which offer the best hope of more lasting jobs in future years.

To do that we must learn the lessons of the past in order to avoid the mistakes that led to the increase of inflation and unemployment in the first place. Today's unemployment is partly due to the sharp increase in oil prices; it absorbed money that might otherwise have gone to increased investment or to buying the things which British factories produce. But that is not all. Too much of our present unemployment is due to enormous past wage increases unmatched by higher output, to union restrictive practices, to overmanning, to strikes, to indifferent management, and to the mistaken belief that, come what may, the Government would always step in to bail out companies in difficulty. No policy can succeed that shirks those basic issues.

We have to earn our living in a world which can choose between the goods we produce and those of other countries. The irony is that many of our people spend five days of the week making British goods and on Saturday go out and spend their earnings on goods produced abroad, goods made in countries which have embraced more modern technology and where management and workforce understand that they are on the same side.

However much we may explain what has led to it, we cannot alter the fact that many people who worked loyally and well for firms up and down the country feel bruised and resentful when, after long and devoted service, they suddenly find themselves without a job.

I understand this. I would feel the same. But that would make it even more inexcusable if any Minister, let alone the Prime Minister, were to deceive them with false hopes or spurious remedies. We are dealing with one of the most complex and sensitive problems of our time and neither rhetoric nor compassion is enough, and demonstrating will not help either.

There have been many voices in the past few weeks calling on us to spend our way back towards a higher level of employment and to cut interest rates at the same time. It is a familiar treatment, and it has been tried by many different governments these past thirty years.

In the early days it worked well enough. In the 1950s a few million pounds of what we learned to call reflation earned a swift reward in jobs and output. But, as time went on, the dose required grew larger and the stimulus achieved grew less. By the 1960s it was needing hundreds of million of extra spending to lift some hundreds of thousands of our people back into employment. By the 1970s we found that after thousands of extra millions had been spent we still had unemployment at levels which ten or twenty years before would have been unthinkable. The trick had been tried too often. The people, as earners and consumers, had rumbled what the Government was doing to their money. They knew the Government was creating inflation and they took that into account in their wage demands. So all the extra money went into wages and prices, and not into more jobs.

So today, if we were to heed the calls to add another thousand million pounds to our plans for spending, we might thereby create an extra 50,000 jobs in two years' time, and even those would be all too swiftly cancelled out by the loss of other jobs in private industry as the result of what we had done.

The fact is that a good chunk of the higher taxes and the higher interest rates needed to find the money for the extra spending would come from the tills of every business in the land. 'Ah', but we are told, 'don't put up the taxes or the interest rates – put them down instead'. In other words, 'print the money'. That way, I must tell you, lies a collapse of trust in sterling both at home and abroad, lies the destruction of the savings of every family. It would lead to suitcase money and penury as the sole reward for thrift. That is not what this Government was elected to do.

But these problems are not peculiar to Britain. Governments all over the world are seeking to borrow on a scale hitherto unknown, and that is why interest rates in every major financial centre have been rising steeply. Indeed, if we had been members of the European Monetary System we might very well have found our interest rates going up long before this September.

That is why it is not a question of choosing between the conquest of inflation and the conquest of unemployment. Indeed, as one of our speakers reminded us yesterday, we are fighting unemployment by fighting inflation. Of course there are those who promise success without tears. I wish they were right. Who more than the Prime Minister would benefit from an easy answer to our troubles?

But if there were a way of beating inflation and unemployment by displeasing no one in the meantime I should take it like a shot. I can tell you unhesitatingly that if I thought Britain could solve her problems more easily, if I found that world conditions opened up a less rugged road, I should not hesitate to take it. There would be no question of sticking doggedly to so-called dogma. I do not want to prove anything, except that Britain can once again succeed and that all of us can share in the fruits of that success.

But I cannot bow to the pressures to take a route which I know will lead us even further from that prospect. That is not obstinacy. It is sheer common sense. The tough measures that this Government have had to introduce are the very minimum needed for us to win through. I will not change just to court popularity. Indeed, if ever a Conservative Government start to do what they know to be wrong because they are afraid to do what they are sure is right, then is the time for Tories to cry 'stop'. But you will never need to do that while I am Prime Minister.

In the teeth of international competition British business is beginning to win the major orders that for too long went elsewhere. £1,000 million of British goods are sold abroad every week. In the last month alone Standard Telephones has won the £170 million contract for a telephone cable right across the Pacific from Australia to Canada – the largest contract that has ever been put out to tender. British Steel has gained contracts worth £70 million in the North Sea and across the world in Hong Kong. The Davy Corporation leads the international consortium to build the £1,250 million steelworks for India. Foster Wheeler has started work on a £140 million petro-chemical plant in Greece. Great international companies like Texas Instruments, Hewlett Packard and Motorola are demonstrating their faith in Britain's future by choosing this country under a Conservative Government as the main location for their expansion.

This is the way to get extra jobs – thousands of extra jobs for Britain. That is the real recovery. And it is happening now. We are winning through.

These are the headline-catching stories, but every bit as important to this Government is the health of the many small and thrusting businesses. We have already taken some sixty measures of direct practical help for small businesses. Indeed, our business start-up scheme is one of the most radical and effective in the Western world. Ten thousand new businesses are starting every month. From them will come so much of the new and lasting employment of the future. I salute their work and their enterprise, and we all wish them well.

But private business is still being held to ransom by the giant monopolist nationalised industries. They do not price themselves on to the dole queues. They do that to other people. They do not have to match the competition. They have captive markets at their beck and call. While free enterprise prices are going up in single figures, prices in the nationalised industries are going up by twenty per cent.

The fact is that only when we introduce the spur of competition in the State-owned industries, do they begin to respond to the needs of the customer. That is why, for example, Norman Fowler, when he was at the Ministry of Transport, stripped away the veto powers of British Rail on bus coach licences. If you can travel now from Manchester to London or from Edinburgh to Bristol by road or rail at fares lower than when we took office, that is thanks to Norman Fowler, just as it is thanks to Freddie Laker that you can cross the Atlantic for so much less than it would have cost you in the early 1970s. Competition works.

You heard Patrick Jenkin [then Industry Secretary] speak of companies as different as Cable and Wireless and British Transport Hotels. I never thought that we should be able to make so much progress with denationalisation in these first two and a half years. And I can assure you that there will be more of these measures in the next session of Parliament. If this is dogmatism then it is the dogmatism of Mr Marks and Mr Spencer, and I'll plead guilty to that any day of the week.

But the thought does sometimes occur to me: if only we had never had all those nice Labour moderates – the sort that now join the SDP – we should never have had these problems in the first place. For it was the Labour moderates who nationalised those industries. They are the guilty men. And they have now shacked up with David Steel – although I do not think that Mr Gladstone would have put it in quite those words. The Liberal leader seems to have quite a passion for pacts, associations, understandings and alliances – a sort of man for all fusions. But, of course there is nothing wrong with pacts provided they are based on a broad identity of principle. But without any genuine common ground parties that cannot advance on their own two feet tend to be trodden on by their partners.

The marriage is for one election only. After that either party can call it a day and go its separate way. Well, of course, nothing is for ever. But it is an odd couple that pencils in a date for divorce before they have even sat down to the wedding breakfast. Perhaps the caution is understandable. Little is known about the SDP, except that its four leaders were senior members of Labour cabinets of the 1960s and 1970s. And if the country is in difficulty today they played their part in bringing that difficulty about. And they have not repudiated their Socialism. Mr Jenkins may remark that, good Lord, he has not used the word 'Socialism' for years, but he has not disowned it. Nor have his former Cabinet colleagues, the other leaders of the new party, whom the Liberals are being asked to embrace.

At a time of growing danger for all who cherish and believe in freedom this party of the soft centre is no shield, no refuge and no answer. As Quintin Hailsham said so vividly a few days ago, 'In a confrontation with the politics of power, the soft centre has always melted away.' And when the soft centre SDP has melted away we are left with the hard shell of the Labour Party.

And make no mistake, the leadership of the Labour Party wants what it has always wanted, the full-blooded Socialism that has been the driving force and purpose of its political life and leadership.

Mr Wedgwood Benn says that 'The forces of Socialism in Britain cannot be stopped.' They can be and they will be. We shall stop them. We shall stop them democratically, and I use the word in the dictionary sense, not the Bennite sense. What they cannot be is half stopped, least of all by those who for years helped to nurture and support them.

Some of the most important things in life are beyond economics. Last Sunday I visited the victims of the IRA bomb outrage in Chelsea, the kind of outrage that has occurred time and again in Northern Ireland. After seeing the injured children and young soldiers, the heartbreak of their parents and wives, one began to count one's blessings. For their world had been suddenly and cruelly shattered by the bombers and terrorists who are the enemies of civilised society everywhere.

We are all in it together, because a breakdown of law and order strikes at everyone. No one is exempt when the terrorists and the bully boys take over. We look to the police and to the courts to protect the freedom of ordinary people, because without order none of us can go about our daily business in safety. Without order fear becomes master, and the strong and violent become a power in the land. This was why the first action after the riots in Brixton and Toxteth was to restore order. Nothing, but nothing, could justify the violence that we saw that week.

I listened to every word of the debate [on law and order] on Tuesday. You made your views absolutely plain. Much as we are doing to support the police and uphold the rule of law you urge us to do even more. I will give you this pledge. Above all other things this Government are determined to maintain order and uphold the Queen's peace. Order depends upon discipline, overwhelmingly upon self-discipline. It is lamentable that the virtues of self-discipline and self-restraint that mark a mature democracy have lately been so little preached in some homes and schools that they have become so poorly practised in our society.

It is when self-discipline breaks down that society has to impose order. It is in this sense that we Conservatives insist that Government must be strong, strong to uphold the rule of law, strong to maintain order, strong to protect freedom. This was the truth which our ancestors knew well, but which some of our generation have managed to unlearn. What is freedom if it does not include freedom from violence and freedom from intimidation?

One of the most revealing things about the rhetoric of the Left is the almost total absence of any reference to the family. Yet the family is the basic unit of our society and it is in the family that the next generation is nurtured. Our concern is to create a property-owning democracy, and it is therefore a very human concern. It is a natural desire of Conservatives that every family should have a stake in society and that the privilege of a family home should not be restricted to the few. The fact that over 55 per cent own their own homes is a tribute to successive Conservative Governments, each one of which has helped to build the property-owning democracy.

It is now our turn to take a major step towards extending home ownership to many who, until now, have been deliberately excluded. Councils, particularly Socialist councils, have clung to the role of landlord. They love it, because it gives them so much power. So, more than two million families have seen themselves paying rent forever. Petty rules aid restrictions and bring enforced dependence. These are the marks of this last vestige of feudalism in Britain. It is the arrogance of the Socialist creed to insist that they know best. For them, equality of opportunity means their opportunity to make sure that everyone else is equal.

Nowhere is this more true than in education. For every family the chance to give your children a better start than you had is one of the greatest joys. Yet we have been so obsessed with the reorganisation of education and with buildings and equipment that we have failed to concentrate on the quality and content of what is taught in our schools. This is precisely what is of greatest concern to parents, and that is why this Government have given them so much more say in the way schools are run, so much more choice in which school to pick for their children, so much more responsibility for the next generation.

But the best schools, and the best housing and the best education will avail us nothing if we lack the means or the resolve to defend the way of life of our people. For abroad, this is a time of danger. We face in the Soviet Union a power whose declared aim is to 'bury' Western civilisation. Experience has taught us that threats such as we now face do not disappear unless they are met calmly and with ingenuity and strength. We cannot defend ourselves, either in this island or in

Europe, without a close, effective and warm-hearted alliance with the United States. Our friendship with America rests not only on the memory of common dangers jointly faced and of common ancestors. It rests on respect for the same rule of law and representative democracy. Our purpose must be not just to confirm, but to strengthen, a friendship which has twice saved us this century.

Had it not been for the magnanimity of the United States, Europe would not be free today. Nor would the peace have been kept in Europe for what is now thirty-six years. Assuming we hold this peace for eight more years, we shall then have enjoyed a longer time free from European war than for two centuries. What a triumph for the Western alliance.

One thrust of Soviet propaganda is concerned to persuade the world that the West, and the United States in particular, is the arms-monger, not the Soviet Union. Nothing could be further from the truth. But it is not surprising that the Russians have found a ready audience, for none of us has any illusions about the horror of nuclear war and we all shrink from it. However, that should force us to consider what is the most likely way of securing peace. It is precisely because I believe that the unilateralists make war more likely that I seek another way.

Should we more easily get the Soviet side to the table to negotiate disarmament if we ourselves had already renounced nuclear weapons? Why should they negotiate if we had already laid down our arms? Would they follow our example? There are no unilateralists in the Kremlin. Until we negotiate multilateral disarmament we have no choice but to retain sufficient nuclear weapons to make it clear to any would-be aggressor that the consequences of an attack on us would be disastrous for them.

To those who want us to close down the American nuclear bases in this country let me say this. We in Britain cannot honourably shelter under the American nuclear umbrella and simultaneously say to our American friends 'You may defend our homes with your home-based missiles, but you may not base those missiles anywhere near our homes'. The cost of keeping tyranny at bay is high but it must be paid, for the cost of war would be infinitely higher and we should lose everything that was worth while.

It is in this dangerous world that Britain must live. She cannot escape it or retreat into an island bunker. Yet that is precisely what the Labour Party proposes. It has become the 'get out' party – to get out of our defence obligations, get out of our NATO nuclear commitments, and get out of the European Community.

It is in European affairs that the contrast with the Conservatives is particularly marked. When in power Labour did nothing to improve the European Community. In two and a half years this Government have slashed our budget contribution and set the Community on the road to far-reaching reform. It is vital that we get it right. £43 out of every £100 we earn abroad comes from the Common Market. Over two million jobs depend on our trade with Europe, two million jobs which will be put at risk by Britain's withdrawal. And even if we kept two-thirds of our trade with the Common Market after we had flounced out – and that is pretty optimistic – there would be a million more to join the dole queues. That is only the beginning.

American and Japanese firms are coming to this country to build factories and provide jobs for us, so that they can sell to the whole of Europe. If we came out, future investors would not come here. They would go to Germany, France or Greece. Even those who are already here would not be satisfied with a market of fifty million 'cribb'd cabbin'd and confined' by import controls, customs duties and tariffs. They would up sticks and away. They would take their investment, their expansion and their jobs into the rest of Europe.

For the unspoken assumption behind policies of withdrawal from the Community and unilateral disarmament is that others will continue to bear their burdens and pick up ours as well; that others would continue to accept our products, even though we refused to accept theirs; that others would continue to ensure the defence of Europe and provide a shield behind which we could shelter.

What a contemptible policy for Britain. Nothing is beyond this nation. Decline is not inevitable. They say I'm an optimist. Well, in this job you get called all sorts of things. An optimist is one of the nicer ones and I would not deny the label. I remember what our country used to be like and I know what we can become again. But first we must rid ourselves of the idea that the laws of economic gravity can somehow be suspended in our favour, and that what applies to other nations does not apply to ours. We must finally come to accept what in some ways we have not accepted since the war – that although then, we with superb defiance helped the free world to survive, the world has not since then and on that account, owed us a living.

We in the Conservative Party know that you cannot get anything for nothing. We hold to the firm foundation of principle, grounded in common sense, common belief and the common purpose of the British people: the common sense of a people who know that it takes effort to achieve success; the common belief in personal responsibility and the values of a free society; and the common purpose that is determined to win through the difficult days to the victory that comes with unity.

This Government, this Government of principle, are seeking the common consent of the people of Britain to work together for the prosperity that has eluded us for so long. There are those who say our nation no longer has the stomach for the fight. I think I know our people and I know they do.

8

CONSERVATIVE
PARTY CONFERENCE

* BRIGHTON *

8th October 1982

THIS IS NOT going to be a speech about the Falklands campaign, though I would be proud to make one. But I want to say just this, because it is true for all our people: the spirit of the South Atlantic was the spirit of Britain at her best. It has been said that we surprised the world, that British patriotism was rediscovered in those spring days. It was never really lost. But it would be no bad thing if the feeling that swept the country then were to continue to inspire us. For if there was any doubt about the determination of the British people it was removed by the men and women who, a few months ago, brought a renewed sense of pride and self-respect to our country.

They were for the most part young. Let all of us here, and in the wider audience outside, pause and reflect on what we who stayed at home owe to those who sailed and fought, and lived and died – and won. If this is tomorrow's generation, Britain has little to fear in the years to come.

In what by any standards was a remarkable chapter in our island's history, it is they who this year wrote its brightest page. In remembering their heroism, let us not forget the courage shown by those same armed forces nearer home. We see them and the other forces of law and order display these qualities day after day in Northern Ireland. Yes, and even closer at hand. I have seen no more moving sight in the last year than the Blues and Royals bearing their tattered standard proudly past the spot in Hyde Park where their comrades had been murdered in a cruel and cowardly bomb attack only two days before.

Terrorism is a deadly threat to our way of life, and we will not be cowed by it. We will continue to resist it with all our power and to uphold the principles of democratic government.

There have been two other party conferences before this, and perhaps I will have a word to say about them later.

First, I want to come to something that dwarfs party politics – indeed, to an issue that dwarfs every other issue of our time. We have invented weapons powerful enough to destroy the whole world. Others have created political systems evil enough to seek to enslave the whole world. Every free nation must face that threat. Every free nation must strain both to defend its freedom and to ensure the peace of the world.

The first duty of a British Government is the defence of the realm, and we shall discharge that duty. Ever since the war the principal threat to our country's safety has come from the Soviet bloc. Twenty-six years ago the Russians marched into Hungary. Twenty-one years ago they built the Berlin Wall. Fourteen years ago they reconquered Czechoslovakia. Three years ago they entered Afghanistan. Two years ago they began to suppress the first stirrings of freedom in Poland.

They knew the strength of the human spirit. They knew that if freedom were allowed to take root in Poland it would spread across Eastern Europe and perhaps to the Soviet Union itself. They knew that the beginning of freedom spelt the beginning of the end for Communism.

Yet despite these regular reminders of the ruthless actions of the Kremlin there are still those who seem to believe that disarmament by ourselves alone would so impress the Russians that they would obligingly follow suit. But peace, freedom and justice are only to be found where people are prepared to defend them. This Government will give the highest priority to our national defence, both conventional and nuclear.

I want to see nuclear disarmament. I want to see conventional disarmament as well. I remember the atomic bombs that devastated Hiroshima and Nagasaki. I remember, too, the bombs that devastated Coventry and Dresden. The horrors of war are indivisible. We all want peace, but not peace at any price. Peace with justice and freedom.

We seek agreement with the Soviet Union on arms control. We want to reduce the levels of both conventional and nuclear forces. But those reductions must be mutual, they must be balanced and they must be verifiable.

I understand the feelings of the unilateralists. I understand the anxieties of parents with children growing up in the nuclear age. But the fundamental question for all of us is whether unilateral nuclear disarmament would make war less likely.

I have to tell you that it would not. It would make war more likely. Aggressors attack because they think they are going to win, and they are more likely to attack the weak than they are to attack the strong.

The springs of war lie not in arms races, real or imaginary, but in the readiness to use force or threaten force against other nations. Remember what Bismarck said: 'Do I want war? Of course not. I want victory'. The causes of wars in the past have not changed, as we know to our cost. But because Russia and the West know that there can be no victory in nuclear war, for thirty-seven years we have kept the peace in Europe, and that is no mean achievement.

That is why we need nuclear weapons, because having them makes peace more secure. Yet at Blackpool last week, the Labour Party, by a huge majority, adopted a new official defence policy. It went like this: Polaris to be scrapped; Trident to be cancelled; Cruise missiles in service to be removed. It is now clear beyond doubt that given the chance the Labour Party wants, they would dismantle Britain's defences wholesale.

Yet do you remember how Aneurin Bevan pleaded with an earlier Labour Party conference not to send a Labour Foreign Secretary naked into the conference chamber? Well, it is a good thing that there isn't going to be a Labour Foreign Secretary.

Yet the Labour Party wants to keep Britain in NATO, continuing to shelter behind American nuclear weapons – so long as they are not on our soil. What utter hypocrisy. To expect an insurance policy but refuse to pay the premium. There must be millions of Labour supporters who are thoroughly disheartened by what they saw at Blackpool last week. I say to them 'Forget about the Militant Tendency – come over and join the Tory tendency.'

A strong and united Western alliance is a guarantee of our peace and security. It is also a beacon of hope to the oppressed people of the Soviet bloc. Britain is a reliable ally, and with a Conservative Government will always remain so, reliable in NATO, reliable beyond NATO, an ally and a friend to be trusted. And trusted not least by our partners in the European Community. Of course, ancient nations do not always find is easy to live together. Yet our commitment to the Common Market is clear. We are all democratic countries where freedom and the rule of law are basic to our institutions.

At present, as you know, Britain pays quite large sums to Community partners often richer than we ourselves. That is fundamentally unjust. It is also short-sighted. As you know, we have just come to the end of our first three-year arrangement. We shall really have to fight – courteously, of course – to make sure that we have a fair deal for the future. But those who would pull us out of Europe must come to terms with the damage that that would do to our people. Even the threat of withdrawal destroys jobs. Firms that invest in the Common Market often decide to come to Britain. Labour's threat to withdraw makes companies hesitate and look elsewhere. That Labour threat is losing us jobs now.

The great economies of Germany and France, once the engine of growth of the European Community, are struggling with declining output and a growing army of unemployed. Across the Atlantic, the United States, Canada and the countries of Latin America have been faced with the most prolonged slump for fifty years. Even the miracle economies of the Pacific Basin – Japan, Korea, Taiwan, Hong Kong and Singapore – are now being hit.

But the economies of the Eastern bloc are in a far worse state than the West. Poland and Romania are hard-pressed to pay their debts, and the Soviet bloc countries generally are riven with shortages of everything, from seed corn to sewing thread.

None of us foresaw a world recession of such gravity. Last week in Blackpool the Opposition suggested that I, single-handed, had brought it about. What powers they attribute to me. If I had that sort of power I would banish recession forever. We have no time for dreams and delusions. The main culprit, and there are others, is the greatest sustained inflation in modern times. Almost every developed country has suffered from it.

For more than a decade economic growth has been thwarted. For more than a decade savers in America and Europe have been systematically robbed by the steady erosion of their savings and for more than a decade the ranks of the unemployed have swollen in the wake of inflation. In 1979 many of us in Europe began the long hard job of wringing inflation out of the system. But Governments had promised to do this over and over again. When the going got tough they resorted to the printing press. No wonder people became cynical.

Journalists, many but not all of them on the Left, were almost daily predicting U-turns. Some, indeed, confidently went around the bend. Now most commentators, with attitudes varying from awe to rage, recognise that we are sticking to our policy. Oh yes, we have been to the IMF. But unlike the last Government we went not as a nation seeking help but as a country giving help to others – a much more fitting role for Britain. From Socialist supplicant to Conservative contributor.

With inflation falling, interest rates coming down, and honest finance, confidence is returning. In spite of hostilities in the South Atlantic, the exchange rate held steady. What a tribute to the determined and unruffled Chancellorship of Geoffrey Howe. No longer will the saver find his money devalued. No longer shall we have two nations, those who profit from inflation and those who lose by it. No longer will paper booms explode in confetti money.

There is no road to inflation-free prosperity except through our own efforts. Two hundred years ago, Edmund Burke blamed the French revolutionaries for trying everywhere to 'evade and slip aside from difficulty'. He said they had a 'fondness for trickery and short-cuts'. There are just as many evaders and short-cutters around today, in the Labour Party, the SDP and among the Liberals, taken jointly or severally, according to taste. Inflate a little here, expand a little there; it's all so easy. In real life such short cuts often turn out to be dead ends.

In the '50s and '60s the fashion was to say that the long term does not matter very much because, as Maynard Keynes put it, 'in the long run we are all dead.' Anyone who thought like that would never plant a tree. We are in the business of planting trees, for our children and grandchildren or we have no business to be in politics at all. We are not a one generation party. We do not intend to let Britain become a one generation society. Let us not forget the lesson of history. The long term always starts today.

Falling inflation on its own will not ensure growth and jobs. We need other things, too. Whether we like it or not, things are changing. They are changing in technology, as we have seen at this conference, with this lectern, that comes up. We keep abreast of the times. They are changing on the map. Far-away countries scarcely heard of ten years ago now overtake us in our traditional industries. Suddenly we are faced with the need to do everything at once – to wake up, catch up and then overtake, even though the future is as hard to predict as ever.

So we have to look as far into that future as we can, and make sure that all the best talents are free to work at full stretch to help to lead this country into that future. Socialists believe that the State can do this better than individuals. Nothing could be more misguided. They are wrong. We cannot opt out of the technology race and try to stand comfortably aside. If we were to do so we should lose not just particular products but whole industries. We dare not leave our neighbours to inherit the world of the microchip. As one production engineer put it, 'The real threat in new technology is the threat of your worst enemies using it'.

Inflation has not been beaten, even when prices stop rising. It is beaten only when costs stop rising. That makes wage costs vital. Pay must relate to output, as every self-employed person will tell you. In the last five years of the 1970s the amount we in Britain paid ourselves for what we produced went up by nearly 100 per cent. In Germany their increase was only 15 per cent. In Japan there was no increase. Of course Japanese workers got more pay, but only from more output. So, they got the orders and we lost jobs. The CBI put it starkly:

> 'Because we have lost over 10 per cent of the home market to imports and 2 per cent of the world export markets to our competitors in the last 12 years we have lost $1\frac{1}{2}$ million jobs.'

One and a half million jobs through losing a fair chunk of our home market to importers and a fair chunk of our export market to our competitors. There is a challenge to management and unions. Get those markets back and we shall get our jobs back.

In the public sector, as you know the Chancellor of the Exchequer has just announced $3\frac{1}{2}$ per cent more available for next year's public pay bill. Before you say that that is not much just remember, for the German civil service it is not going to be $3\frac{1}{2}$ per cent but 2 per cent. In Japan the Japanese civil servants are getting no rise at all. Maybe that will put the $3\frac{1}{2}$ per cent in perspective.

It is important to keep wage costs down, to accept new technology. But while it is important to do all that, good management and good industrial relations are vital to our future. We heard a lot at Blackpool about how Labour would work with the unions. Of course, they do not really mean that. What they mean is cosy get-togethers at No. 10. That is the old pals' act. It has nothing to do with life on the shop floor and that is where the real problems are sorted out.

When I travel overseas, time and again they say to me, 'Strikes. You have so many strikes. If it were not for that we would give you more contracts. We would invest more in Britain'. In vain do I say that private industry has very few strikes. The fact is that the much publicised disruptions in the public sector do Britain down every time. I only wish that some of those trade union members on strike in the public sector would realise how many jobs their actions lost – not necessarily their own jobs, but the jobs of people in manufacturing industry, whose taxes pay their wages. We cannot say it too often – 'Strikes lose jobs'.

It will take a long time to get employment up sufficiently, to get unemployment down as far as we all want. The task is even harder because we are going through a phase in Britain when the number of people of working age is rising. There are many more young people leaving school and wanting jobs than there are older people reaching retirement. Over a period of eight years there will be $1\frac{1}{4}$ million extra people of working age. Even without the recession we should have needed a lot more new jobs just to stop the number of unemployed rising. That shows the magnitude of the task. Today's unemployed are the victims of yesterday's mistakes.

Government destroyed jobs by fuelling inflation; trade unions destroyed jobs by restrictive practices; militants destroyed jobs by driving customers away. But that is the past and whatever the problems, we have got to tackle them, not with words, not with rhetoric but with action. Rhetoric is easy but it does not produce jobs. Indeed, if rhetoric could cure unemployment we would have jobs galore by this time.

For the future, Norman Tebbit [then Employment Secretary] has told you that every 16-year-old who leaves school next year will either have a job or a year of full time training. Unemployment will not then be an option, and that is right. But a Government cannot do everything.

If we are to beat unemployment, and we must, we have to do it together. The Government are getting inflation down, interest rates down, reforming trade union law, cutting regulations and removing restrictions. The rest is up to industry, the work force and management in partnership. In the end it is private employers who will produce the great majority of jobs.

Time and again history beats out the same message. Competition is better for the consumer than State control. We are acting on that conviction. Three and a half years ago defenders of the status quo tried to brand denationalisation as irrelevant. Now the critics are finding it harder to ignore the evidence of their own eyes. They cannot help seeing the new, long-distance coaches speeding down the motorways, at very much lower fares. They cannot miss the success of Cable and Wireless or British Aerospace. Britoil will be the next to be denationalised and British Telecommunications after that. How absurd it will seem in a few years' time that the State ran Pickford's Removals and Gleneagles Hotel.

We are only in our first term. But already we have done more to roll back the frontiers of Socialism than any previous Conservative Government. In the next Parliament we intend to do a lot more. We are seeing increasing evidence of the savings that can be made. Local authority after local authority has found that even the prospect of contracting out their refuse collection produces amazing economies from their staff. As Dr Johnson nearly said: 'When you know you are going to be privatised in a fortnight it concentrates the mind wonderfully'.

I hope that every Conservative councillor in the land will act on what Councillor Chope of Wandsworth told us. Wandsworth has gone out to private contractors and down have come the rates. And don't we all want that. Where Wandsworth has led, let other Conservative councils follow.

I should like to say a word about the Health Service, because value for money is just as important in the Health Service. Our opponents' picture of us as a party that doesn't care about the Health Service is utterly untrue, and is particularly ridiculous from the Labour Party. When they were in office they had nearly 2,000 fewer hospital doctors and 40,000 fewer nurses than we have and every one of them was then much worse off than today. But that same Labour Party now supports these who are disrupting the National Health Service and lengthening the very waiting lists that we have brought down. What sort of twisted compassion is that?

'I believe that we should condemn industrial action with its damage to the Health Service, whether it comes from doctors, nurses or anyone else who works in the service.' Those aren't my words; those were the Labour Minister of Health's, David Ennals, when he was in office. We supported him because it was true then, and it is true now. We have a magnificent record in the Health Service. We heard that splendid speech from Norman Fowler in one of the best debates in this conference. This year we are spending 5 per cent more in real terms on the Health Service than Labour. So under the Conservatives we have more doctors, more nurses, more money. Hardly the behaviour of a Government bent on destroying the Health Service.

Naturally, we have a duty to make sure that every penny is properly spent, and that is why we are setting up a team to examine the use of manpower in the National Health Service. Naturally we have a duty to do that. It is part of our duty to the taxpayer. Of course we welcome the growth of private health insurance. There is no contradiction between that and supporting the National Health Service. It brings in more money, it helps to reduce the waiting lists, and it stimulates new treatments and techniques.

But let me make one thing absolutely clear. The National Health Service is safe with us. As I said in the House of Commons on December 1 last: 'The principle that adequate health care should be provided for all, regardless of ability to pay, must be the foundation of any arrangement for financing the Health Service'. We stand by that.

It is not only in the National Health Service that our record has been very good.

Next month the old age pension will go up by 11 per cent, and that despite the worst recession since the 1930s. That is some achievement too. Whatever our difficulties, 9 million pensioners have been fully protected from inflation. We gave our promise and we kept it.

We do not measure our success merely by how much money the Government spends. The well-being of our people is about far more than the welfare state. It is about self-reliance, family help, voluntary help as well as State provision. In a society which is truly healthy, responsibility is shared and help is mutual.

Wherever we can we shall extend the opportunity for personal ownership and the self-respect that goes with it. Three hundred and seventy thousand families have now bought their own homes from councils, new towns and housing associations. That is the result of this Government's housing policy carried through in the teeth of opposition from the Labour Party. We have fought them all the way and we won. Half a million more people will now live and grow up as freeholders with a real stake in the country and with something to pass on to their children. There is no prouder word in our history than 'freeholder'.

This is the largest transfer of assets from the State to the family in British history and it was done by a Conservative Government. And this really will be an irreversible shift of power to the people. The Labour Party may huff and puff about putting a stop to the sale of council houses. They may go on making life unpleasant for those who try to take advantage of their legal rights, and what a wicked thing it is to do that. But they do not dare pledge themselves to take those houses back because they know we are right, because they know it is what the people want. And besides, they would be making too many of their own councillors homeless, not to mention one or two of their MPs.

We want to bring more choice to parents, too. We as parents have the prime reponsibility to set the standards and to instil the values by which our children are brought up. None of us has the right to blame the teachers for failing to make up for our shortcomings. But we have every right to be involved in what goes on in our children's schools. As parents we want to be sure not just about the teaching of the three Rs, but about the discipline and about the values by which our children are taught to live. We have given parents more say in the choice of schools. We have put parents on governing bodies. For the first time in modern Britain a Government is really paying attention not just to school organisation, but to the curriculum; not just to the buildings, but to what is taught inside them.

And we are not afraid to talk about discipline and moral values. To us 'Law and Order' is not an election slogan. It is the foundation of the British tradition. I believe that, looking back on this first Parliament of ours, it will be said that we have done more to support the police than any British Government since the war. There are more of them, we pay them better, we train them better and we equip them better, and for that you know who we have to thank. I am eternally grateful for the good sense, good humour and loyalty of Willie Whitelaw. Perhaps only I know how staunch he was throughout the whole of the Falklands Campaign, and the difficult decisions we had to take. Thank you very much.

It cannot be the police alone who are on duty. As parents, as teachers, as politicians and as citizens, what we say and do, whether in the home, the classroom or the House of Commons is bound to leave its mark on the next generation. The television producer who glamourises violence may find his viewing figures ultimately reflected in the crime statistics. And a public figure who comments to the camera on issues of the day should be especially careful of what he says.

The other day, the last Labour Prime Minister – and I do mean 'the last Labour Prime Minister' – spoke of what he called ' a contingent right' in certain circumstances to break the law. None of us has a right, contingent or otherwise, to uphold the law that suits us and to break the one that does not. That way lies anarchy.

There are many people in Britain who share the hopes and the ideals of the Conservative Party. They share our great purpose to restore to this country its influence and self-respect. But they are anxious about the future and uncertain about the changes that we have had to make. They have not recognised how far the debating ground of British politics has moved to the Left over the last thirty years. Where the Left stood yesterday the Centre stands today. Yet the British people have not moved with it. Instinctively they know that we have to pull this country back to the real centre again. But the anxious say to us 'You cannot do everything at once. The recession and the international economic situation make things particularly difficult. Why not adapt your approach a little, give in for the time being until things are getting better and then you can start again after the next election when you have longer time to do it'.

To do that would be a betrayal. People in Britain have grown to understand that this Government will make no false promises, nor will it fail in its resolve. How can the Government urge the people to save and to build for tomorrow if the people know that same Government is willing to bend and trim for the sake of votes today? That is not trusting the people, and it is not the way to be trusted by them. Nothing could be more damaging to our prospects as a nation than for this Government to throw away the reputation it has earned for constancy and resolve. It would throw away three years of hard-won achievement.

On what moral basis would we be entitled to ask for the nation's support next time? The only way we can achieve great things for Britain is by asking great things of Britain. We will not disguise our purpose, nor betray our principles. We will do what must be done. We will tell the people the truth and the people will be our judge.

```
┌─────────────────────────────┐
│   CONSERVATIVE              │
│   PARTY CONFERENCE         │
│   ─────────────────        │
│   * BLACKPOOL *            │
│   ─────────────────        │
│   14th October 1983        │
└─────────────────────────────┘
```

WE MEET in the aftermath of a general election. I think we can say that the result was not exactly a photo-finish. We are grateful for victory. We are grateful to you and the thousands of people in every part of the country who worked so hard to ensure success. We thank you all. And we do not forget today the man who so brilliantly organised the campaign [Cecil Parkinson].

Last June we again won the honour to serve the British people. How best shall we do it? Not by being complacent about our majority nor by assuming that our past achievements will automatically bring us future success. Our first four years were the preparation for further action. Further action there will be. When we were first elected in May 1979, it was to tackle the real problems which others had shirked. We did tackle them. Anyone who understood those problems never expected them to be solved in the space of one Parliament. But we have made a start. And we shall see it through.

We were elected to bring inflation down; we brought it down. It was, and still is, a series of continuing battles which commands our unremitting effort. The pessimists told us it could not be done. They under-estimated three things: this Government, you, Mr President [Sir Geoffrey Howe], and the British people.

We were elected to reform the trade unions. With the support of millions of trade unionists we have passed two major Acts of Parliament. And what a lot we owe to Norman Tebbit [as Employment Secretary]. But there is a lot more to do – a great deal more, and you can rely on us to do it.

We were elected to extend home ownership and we gave council tenants the right to buy their own homes. And never let it be forgotten that Labour fought it tooth and nail, in their local councils, in Parliament and through the courts. It was not part of their philosophy that council tenants should acquire the rights and dignity of freeholders. It is because of Conservative conviction and persistence that nearly three-quarters of a million more council tenants have either bought or are buying their homes. And with Ian Gow as Minister of Housing there will be many, many more.

We were elected to reduce direct taxation. We have reduced the rates of income tax and we have raised the thresholds. But there are still too many people paying income tax and the burden is still too great. The fight for lower taxes will go on and no one will fight harder to bring them down than our new Chancellor of the Exchequer, Nigel Lawson.

We were elected to strengthen the forces of law and order. Thanks to Willie Whitelaw [as Home Secretary] there are now more policemen, better paid, better equiped than ever before – and more of them back on the beat. But, as you heard from Leon Brittan [the new Home Secretary], this Government is reinforcing its efforts. But it is not just a case of 'Leave it to Leon'. Law and order is not just his problem. It involves every citizen in the land. None of us can opt out.

We were elected with a clear commitment to the European Community and to fight tenaciously for British interests within it. We have honoured that commitment. We have both fought for our interests and extended our influence. But we are not half-hearted members of the Community. We are in. And we are in to stay. And I look forward to another famous victory in the European elections next June.

We were elected to secure the defence of the realm. We have made clear, through word and deed, to friend and foe alike, our resolve to keep Britain strong and free. No one doubts now that this country under this Government stands shoulder to shoulder with her allies to defend the cause of justice and freedom, and to work together for peace. Under Michael Heseltine's vigorous leadership [as Defence Secretary], we won the argument against one-sided nuclear disarmament. That is the record we put before the British people at the General Election. They are the ultimate jury and they found in our favour. These things were achieved by strong government. Strong to do what only governments can do. But a strong government knows where to draw the line. It has confidence to trust the people. And a free people know that the power of government must be limited. That trust and that confidence are the hallmark of the Government which was re-elected on 9th June.

At that election, Socialism offered yesterday's policies for today's problems. Socialism was routed. The other day at Brighton they were given a re-spray, polished and offered once again to the people. But they are still yesterday's policies – and even yesterday they did not work. Our people will never 'Keep the red flag flying here'. There is only one banner that Britain flies – the one that has kept flying for centuries – the red, white and blue.

One of the great debates of our time is about how much of your money should be spent by the State and how much you should keep to spend on your family. Let us never forget this fundamental truth: the State has no source of money other than money which people earn themselves. If the State wishes to spend more, it can do so only by borrowing your savings, or by taxing you more. It is no good thinking that someone else will pay. That 'someone else' is you. There is no such thing as public money. There is only taxpayers' money. Prosperity will not come by inventing more and more lavish public expenditure programmes. You do not grow richer by ordering another cheque book from the bank.

No nation ever grew more prosperous by taxing its citizens beyond their capacity to pay. We have a duty to make sure that every penny-piece we raise in taxation is spent wisely and well. For it is our Party which is dedicated to good housekeeping. Indeed, I would not mind betting that if Mr Gladstone were alive today, he would apply to join the Conservative Party.

Protecting the taxpayer's purse. Protecting the public services. These are our two great tasks and their demands have to be reconciled. How very pleasant it would be, how very popular it would be, to say: 'Spend more on this, expand more on that'. We all have our favourite causes – I know I do. But someone has to add up the figures. Every business has to do it. Every housewife has to do it. Every Government should do it. And this one will.

But throughout history, clever men – some of them economists, not all of them rascals but few of them businessmen – have tried to show that the principles of prudent finance do not really apply to this Government, this budget, that institution. Not so. They always do. And every sensible person knows it, no one better than you, Mr President, who had to deal with countries which flouted those principles and are now up to their eyes in debt. Who do they turn to? Those who follow prudent principles like us. When there is only so much money to spend, you have to make choices. And the same is true of government.

It is sometimes suggested that governments can opt out of these choices. They cannot. Let me for a moment take the subject which we have so much debated, the Health Service. People talk about a free service. It is not free. You have to pay for it. Five years ago, just before I came into Number Ten, a family of four was having to pay, on average, through various taxes, some £560 a year for the Health Service. This year, that same family will have to pay £1,140 a year – more than double. Let me put it another way. This year the Health Service is costing over £15,000 million – half the total yield of income tax.

The Health Service has one million employees. It is the largest employer in Europe. It really is our job to see that it is managed properly. I pay tribute, as we all do, to those doctors, nurses and others who work so hard to keep up the standards of care. We are all thankful for the great advances in public health since the war – the continuing decline in child mortality, the virtual eradication of diseases like diptheria and TB, the miraculous new techniques of surgery. But every human institution can be improved. I reject totally the Socialist view that the most efficient organisation is the one that employs the largest number.

Now let me get one or two things through about that budget. Let me put the facts on record just a little bit more. The Health Service budget is very large. We are not cutting it. We are keeping to the plans we announced before the Election. And which I repeated as a pledge during the campaign. I will say it again. We are spending £700 million more on health this year alone, another £800 million next year, and a further £700 million the year after that. That is the pledge I made and that is the pledge that will be kept. And we have to keep within that huge budget. That is what good management means and that is what we are doing – as Norman Fowler [the Social Services Secretary] explained in his outstanding speech yesterday morning.

Of course, our opponents who could never begin to match our record are once again trying to pin on us all the adjectives in the dictionary of denigration – harsh, uncaring, uncompassionate and the rest. I am told that the new Leader of Her Majesty's Opposition – and long may he hold that office – went so far as to say at Brighton last week that I was engaged in 'terminating the Health Service'. Let me tell you how you really terminate the Health Service. You do it by pretending there are no hard choices; you do it by behaving as though Britain has a bottomless purse; you do it by promising what you cannot deliver; by assuming that all you need to do it to snap your fingers, cry 'abracadabra', and lo and behold the sky's the limit. But the sky is not the limit, for this or any other Government, or indeed for any other country, and to imply that it is or ever can be, is sheer humbug and a fraud on the people. Our opponents would spend, spend and spend before they had even filled in the coupon, let alone won the pools.

At this conference last year, you may remember that I said: 'The NHS is safe with us'. I will go further. The NHS is safe only with us because only this Government will see that it is prudently managed and financed, and that care is concentrated on the patient rather than on the bureaucrat. That is the true and the genuine caring.

When our opponents start demanding more spending on hospitals, schools, roads, or for the old folk, I do not hear them at the same time calling for more income tax, or an extra 5 per cent on VAT, or even more on local authority rates. In facing up to this problem of controlling public expenditure, we in Britain are far from alone. Let me give you one or two examples of what is happening in other countries. In Socialist France, they have introduced boarding charges for hospital patients. The French and the West Germans have delayed pension increases and are cutting unemployment benefit. In Holland they are cutting social security benefits and the pay of the public service by $3\frac{1}{2}$ per cent. In Belgium and Denmark they have de-indexed social security benefits. Think what people would say in this country had we done some of those things. I do not say that those measures are the ones we should follow but I do say that no government, whatever its political complexion, can suspend the laws of arithmetic or run away from reality.

There is something else we share with other nations. The world recession has brought high unemployment to almost every country. In such times, people understandably ask: where will the new jobs come from? There is always a temptation to believe that the dynamism of the past will be exhausted and that the best we can hope for is to share out the work we have already got. Nothing could be more mistaken: that is not how our fathers and grandfathers transformed the standard of living in the Western world. They did not wait for the boost or scan the horizon for the upturn. They were the upturn and they provided the boost themselves.

If Britain had stayed as it was in 1900, millions of people in this country would still be working in agriculture and domestic service would still be at 1900 levels. If people had known then that by 1983 less than three per cent of the population would be in agriculture and only a tiny fraction in domestic service, they would surely have asked: 'Where will the other millions find jobs?' Who could have foretold then what people would want today, and what they would buy today? Who could have foretold then what inventiveness would produce decades hence? While some machines that were invented replaced unskilled work, others created new goods undreamed of – motor cars, kitchen equipment, new fabrics, films – and those created, those new machines, thousands of jobs.

But as new industries sprang into being, the old ones declined, causing unhappiness and hardship. We did not then have the means or the organisation to temper the winds of change – the cash benefits, the re-training schemes, the redundancy benefits, that we have now. Tories have long been prominent in creating those schemes and benefits. Again and again, Tory Governments took the lead: in extending unemployment insurance, in providing compensation for past industrial injury and disease, and in bringing in training schemes for the future. In the declining industries, we have made available compensation on a uniquely generous scale for those who have had to lose their jobs. Let no one accuse this Party or this Government of failing to care about the unemployed.

This Government has also taken two very far-reaching steps to see that Britain is never again left unprepared for technological change. Our Youth Training Scheme is the most imaginative in the Western world. And when it is well under way, every 16-year-old will have the choice either to stay on at school, or to find a job, or to receive training. At that age, unemployment should not be an option. That is our objective. We are responding to the needs of industry by reintroducing technical training into our schools. And not a moment too soon.

This Government is building for the future. We all want a higher standard of living – as individuals and as a community. The same is true in other countries. The challenge we face is not one of sharing out the limited amount of work like spreading butter thinly on a slice of bread. It is how to translate our wants and aspirations into work to be done by our people. It is by producing what people want to buy that unemployment will be solved.

The same drive and inventiveness that created the great industries of the past and brought prosperity to our people are still at work today. New industries are still being born. New products are still coming on to the market. New services are still developing. Only last month, I opened the largest oil production platform in the North Sea. Fifteen years ago, the oil and gas industry, the offshore industry, employed only a handful of people. Today, it employs more than 100,000.

Who, ten or twenty years ago, could have foretold that so many homes would have video recorders – which we are just beginning to produce here – music centres, home computers and pocket calculators? Who would have foreseen the revolution in office equipment and information technology? These may be called light industries, but they produce tens of thousands of solid new jobs.

In service industries too, the past ten years have seen some of the most rapid increases in jobs. Let me give you a few examples because I know you are still wondering where the new jobs are going to come from and I am trying to show you they have come from new machinery and new technology in the past and that is still happening today. Let us have a look at the new service industries and see what has happened recently. Over 300,000 more jobs have been created in insurance, banking and finance than there were ten years ago. There are over 600,000 more jobs in the scientific and professional services, over 200,000 more jobs in hotels and catering and nearly 60,000 more jobs in sports and other recreations. All of those are service jobs for skilled and unskilled workers alike. So, as we have redundancies in the declining industries we are getting new jobs in the new industries, new jobs in some of the older industries that are modernising themselves, and new jobs in some of the service industries. They are being created by our dynamic economy of today.

Let us not belittle our achievements. There must be quite a lot right about a country that can sell 30 per cent of its output in the teeth of fierce competition. And this is a country that can still export £1,000 million worth of goods every week, without counting oil. Which is the second biggest exporter of services in the world – second to the United States? It is Britain. So let us send our warm thanks and congratulations to all of those whose splendid achievements are bearing such fruit.

But, although it is a marvellous record, we have to remember something else. Our competitors are improving all the time. And some of them started well ahead of us. So we must improve even faster than they do if we are to catch up. It is no good just beating our previous best; we have to beat our competitors. That means that our Government must not put a heavier burden on our industry than other governments place on theirs.

What does that mean? I will tell you. It means we must stick to the policies that get inflation down and interest rates down, which keep business taxes down, and local rates down, policies that cut through the thicket of restrictions and policies that will reduce the time taken for planning permission. It is important that we continue with each and every one. If Atlas carries the world on his shoulders, we need a good strong Atlas – and not too heavy a world. Our job in Government is to provide the right framework in which enterprise can flourish. And we are doing it.

But, of course, it rests with the people themselves to pick up the challenge. And it is in the people that we Conservatives place our trust. The great surges of progress and prosperity in this country did not come directly from Government action. They were not based on national plans. They came from free men, working in a free society, where they could deploy their talents to their best advantage, for themselves, for their countries and for the future. That is our policy. It has worked in the past and it will work again. It is to achieve a new prosperity and the new jobs for our people in the future.

The first duty of Government is to make our future and our way of life secure. In the election campaign, it became clear that the overwhelming majority of our people were determined to see that our country was properly defended. They recognised that Britain's possession of nuclear weapons has helped to prevent not only nuclear war but conventional war too. Those of our opponents who said the opposite hastily had to pretend that they did not really mean what they said. Those of our friends overseas who might have doubted the resolve of the British people were reassured by our victory.

To retain peace with freedom and justice we must maintain the unity of NATO. Most of our people would never vote for a party that undermines NATO and snipes at our allies. The so-called peace movement may claim to be campaigning for peace but it is NATO and the Western Alliance which have been delivering peace in Europe for more than thirty years. Peace does not come by chanting the word like some mystical incantation. It comes from that ceaseless vigilance which the Western Allies have sustained for nearly two generations. Peace is hard work, and we must not allow people to forget it.

The Soviet challenge remains. To say that is not to welcome the fact and still less to take pleasure in it. But if we are properly to defend ourselves, we must first make a realistic assessment of the threat we face. No one can wish away the post-war history of the Soviet use of force, nor wipe out the grim calendar of Soviet suppression of freedom. You know the calendar almost as well as I do: 1953, East Germany; 1956, Hungary; 1961, The Berlin Wall; 1968, Czechoslovakia; 1979, Afghanistan; 1981, Poland; 1983, The South Korean Civil Airliner.

The Soviet Union is unlikely to change much, or quickly. Internal difficulties will not necessarily soften its attitudes. Nor should we overestimate the influence of the West on that vast suspicious country. Its leaders are likely to remain distrustful and hostile to the West and ruthless in their international deeds.

Economically, of course, you may say, we have nothing to fear. Whatever the difficulties, economies that flourish do so under the banner of the market and not of Marx. In the battle of ideas, the Soviet Union are in retreat as more and more peoples in Africa and Asia discover what Europe has already discovered – the cruel emptiness of Marxism. And, you know, the Russian leaders know this. Why else do they prevent their people from travelling freely? Why else do they jam Western broadcasts? Why else do they lock away those of their fellow citizens who have the temerity to ask that the Soviet Union should abide by its undertakings at Helsinki?

But whatever we think of the Soviet Union, Soviet Communism cannot be disinvented. We have to live together on the same planet and that is why, when the circumstances are right, we must be ready to talk to the Soviet leadership: that is why we should grasp every genuine opportunity for dialogue and keep that dialogue going in the interests of East and West alike. But such exchanges must be hard-headed. We do not want the word 'dialogue' to become suspect in the way the word 'detente' now is.

A major element in that dialogue must be arms control – indeed we in the Western world would like to have arms reduction, provided always that the balance is kept and the undertakings to reduce or destroy weapons can be verified. Arms reduction in those circumstances, on those grounds. That is our aim. I think it is important that we understand exactly what kind of negotiations are going on in Geneva. We are negotiating about two classes of nuclear weapons, the intermediate weapons and also the long-range strategic missiles. Two sets of negotiations. Let me talk about the intermediate weapons first.

Some six years ago the Soviet Union began to replace hers by the more accurate SS 20s which have three times as many warheads. We had nothing comparable, so NATO in 1979 decided to modernise our intermediate weapons with Cruise and Pershing II missiles in order to restore the balance. But at the same time we tried to persuade the Soviet Union to reduce the number of SS 20s. There was no response. Then we offered to eliminate our missiles if they would eliminate theirs. If they agreed, no Cruise or Pershing II missiles would be deployed. That is President Reagan's zero-option. Still there has been no positive response from the Soviet Union. And all the signs are that there will not be. In that case, the first Cruise and Pershing II missiles will be deployed at the end of this year. Nevertheless in Geneva we shall persist in our efforts for an agreement to keep the numbers as low as possible on both sides. No weapons would be better than some. But few would be better than more.

Meanwhile the whole situation has been deliberately clouded and confused by the Soviet propaganda attempt to suggest that our strategic weapon, Polaris, should be included in the intermediate weapon talks. Now Polaris is our last resort deterrent. We had it long before the SS 20s and then, and now, we need it, in case we should ever be threatened by Russia's great arsenal of strategic weapons. And however you measure it our strategic force amounts to only $2\frac{1}{2}$ per cent of theirs; forty of theirs to every one of ours.

But there are separate talks in Geneva concerning strategic weapons. The Soviet Union and the United States have some 9,000 warheads each. In 1981, President Reagan suggested that, as a first step, the missile warheads should be cut on both sides by one-third. Once again there has been no positive response from the Soviet Union. But if ever this enormous strategic armoury were drastically reduced, then of course we should wish to consider how we in Britain could contribute to the arms control process.

The West has made proposal after proposal for arms reduction. And the day the leaders of the Soviet Union genuinely decide that they want, through arms control agreements, to make this a safer world, they will be pushing at an open door. Until then our threefold policy will be the same – realistically to assess the potential aggressor, firmly to maintain our capacity to defend and deter, and always to stand ready to talk. As I am sure you will understand, there is no one more anxious for genuine disarmament than the person who bears the ultimate responsibility for the nuclear deterrent in our own country. I wanted to say that to you. You will understand how important it is to me that we try to make those arms reduction talks succeed.

We won a great election victory on 9th June and there is no reason on earth why we should not take pleasure in that alone, but I really believe that we have done more than that.

The Election showed that something remarkable has happened in this country. And our opponents were just as aware of it as those millions of people who supported us. What I think we discovered and expressed, both in our four years of Government and in the programme which grew out of those four years was where the heart of the British people lies. We are a mature nation which through centuries of trial, sorrow and achievement has developed a common view of life.

There are things for which we as a people have stood for centuries: the will and capacity to defend our way of life; the rule of law; the belief in private property and home ownership; the protection of the elderly and the sick; the limitation of Government; and the freedom of the individual. By giving voice to these convictions in 1979, by holding fast to them for four years, by having them reaffirmed in 1983, I believe we have altered the whole course of British politics for at least a generation.

We have created the new common ground and that is why our opponents have been forced to shift their ground. Both the policy and direction of State Socialism on which they have been fighting for years have been utterly rejected by our people. State Socialism is not in the character of the British people. It has no place in our traditions. It has no hold on our hearts. A Socialist Party can only hope to survive in Britain by pretending that it is something else. We are told the Labour Party is reassessing its attitude to home ownership and is thinking again about Europe. We are told the Social Democrats now sing the virtues of capitalism, competition and the customer.

We have entered a new era. The Conservative Party has staked out the common ground and the other parties are tiptoeing on to it. The Conservative Party has a greater responsibility than ever before. Now, more than ever, we draw our support from all sections of the nation. It is our pride and our purpose to strive always to be a national party – a party which speaks for and to the whole nation.

In 1975, standing where I am standing today, I said that I had a vision for Britain: a Britain strong in the defence of peace and justice; a Britain strong in support of personal freedom; a Government strong enough to protect the weak; but a Government with the strength to allow people to lead their own lives. Visions do not become a reality overnight – or even in four years. They have to be worked for, consistently, unswervingly.

We have set a true course – a course that is right for the character of Britain, right for the people of Britain and right for the future of Britain. To that course we shall hold fast. We shall see it through – to success.

10

CONSERVATIVE
PARTY CONFERENCE

* BRIGHTON *

12th October 1984

THE BOMB ATTACK on the Grand Hotel early this morning was first and foremost an inhuman, undiscriminating attempt to massacre innocent, unsuspecting men and women staying in Brighton for our Conservative conference. Our first thoughts must at once be for those who died and for those who are now in hospital recovering from their injuries.

But the bomb attack clearly signified more than this. It was an attempt not only to disrupt and terminate our conference; it was an attempt to cripple Her Majesty's democratically-elected Government. That is the scale of the outrage in which we have all shared, and the fact that we are gathered here now, shocked but composed and determined, is a sign not only that this attack has failed but that all attempts to destroy democracy by terrorism will fail.

I should like to express our deep gratitude to the police, firemen, ambulancemen, nurses and doctors, to all the emergency services, and to the staff of the hotel, to our ministerial staff and the Conservative Party staff who stood with us and shared the danger.

As Prime Minister and Leader of the Party I thank them all and send our heartfelt sympathy to all those who have suffered.

Now it must be business as usual. We must go on to discuss the things we have talked about during this conference, one or two matters of foreign affairs and after that two subjects I have selected for special consideration, unemployment and the miners' strike.

This conference has been superbly chaired – and our Chairman came on this morning with very little sleep and carried on marvellously. The conference, with excellent contributions from our members, has been an outstanding example of orderly assembly and free speech. We have debated the great national and international issues as well as those which affect the daily lives of our people. We have seen at the rostrum miner and pensioner, nurse and manager, clergyman and student.

In Government we have been fulfilling the promises contained in our election manifesto which was put to the people in a national ballot. This Government is reasserting Parliament's ultimate responsibility for controlling the total burden of taxation on our citizens, whether levied by central or local government. And in the coming session of Parliament we shall introduce legislation which will abolish the GLC and the metropolitan county councils.

In the quest for sound local government we rely on the help of Conservative councillors. Their task should never be underestimated and their virtues should not go unsung. They work hard and conscientiously with a true spirit of service. I pay special tribute to the spendid efforts of Conservative councils up and down the country in getting better value for money through greater efficiency and putting out work to competitive tender. This is privatisation at the local level and we need more of it.

At national level, since the general election just over a year ago, the Government has denationalised five major enterprises, making a total of thirteen since 1979. Yesterday, you gave Norman Tebbit a standing ovation. Today our thoughts are with him and his family.

Again and again denationalisation has brought greater motivation to managers and workforce, higher profits and rising investment. What is more, many in industry now have a share of the firm for which they work. We Conservatives want every owner to be an earner and every earner to be an owner. Soon we shall have the biggest-ever act of denationalisation with British Telecom, and British Airways will follow. And we have not finished yet. There will be more to come in this Parliament.

Just as we have stood by our pledge on denationalisation it is our pride that despite the recession we have kept faith with nine million pensioners. Moreover, by keeping inflation down we have protected the value of their savings. As Norman Fowler told the conference on Wednesday, this Government has not only put more into pensions but has increased resources for the National Health Services. Our record for last year, to be published shortly, will show that the Health Service today is providing more care, more services, and more help for the patient than at any stage in its history. That is Conservative care in practice. I think that it is further proof of the statement I made in Brighton in this hall two years ago. Perhaps some of you remember it. 'The National Health Service is safe with us'.

This performance in the social services could never have been achieved without an efficient and competitive industry to create the wealth we need. Efficiency is not the enemy, but the ally of compassion.

In our discussions here we have spoken of the need for enterprise, profits, and a wider distribution of property among all the people. In the Conservative Party we have no truck with outmoded Marxist doctrine about class warfare. For us, it is not who you are, who your family is, or where you come from that matters. It is what you are and what you can do for our country that counts. That is our vision. It is a vision worth defending and we shall defend it. Indeed, this Government will never put the defence of our country at risk.

No one in their senses wants nuclear weapons for their own sake. But equally no responsible Prime Minister could take the colossal gamble of giving up our nuclear defences while our greatest potential enemy kept theirs. Policies which would throw out all American nuclear bases – bases which have been here since the time of Mr Attlee, President Truman and Sir Winston Churchill – would wreck NATO and leave us totally isolated from our friends in the United States – and friends they are. No nation in history has ever shouldered a greater burden, or shouldered it more willingly nor more generously, than the United States. This party is pro-American.

We must constantly remind people what the defence policy of the Opposition party would mean. Their idea that by giving up our nuclear deterrent we could somehow escape the result of a nuclear war elsewhere is nonsense. And it is a delusion to assume that conventional weapons are a sufficient defence against nuclear attack. And do not let anyone slip into the habit of thinking that conventional war in Europe is some kind of comfortable option. With the huge array of modern weapons held by the Soviet Union, including chemical weapons in large quantities, it would be a cruel and terrible conflict. The truth is that possession of the nuclear deterrent has prevented not only nuclear war but also conventional war. And to us, peace is precious beyond price. We are the true peace party.

The nuclear deterrent has not only kept the peace but it will continue to preserve our independence. Winston Churchill's warning is just as true now as when he made it many, many years ago. He said:

'Once you take the position of not being able in any circumstances to defend your rights against . . . agression . . . there is no end to the demands that will be made or the humiliations that must be accepted.'

He knew, and we must heed his warning. Yet Labour's defence policy remains: no Polaris, no Cruise missiles in Britain, no United States nuclear bases in Britain, no Trident, no independent nuclear deterrent. There is I think just one answer the nation will give – no defence, no Labour Government.

In foreign affairs this year has seen two major diplomatic successes. We have reached a detailed and binding agreement with China on the future of Hong Kong. It is an agreement designed to preserve Hong Kong's flourishing economy and unique way of life. We believe that it meets the needs and wishes of the people of Hong Kong themselves.

A few weeks ago the unofficial members of the Executive Council of Hong Kong came to see me. We kept in touch with them the whole time and they have frequently made journeys to No. 10 Downing Street as the negotiations with China have proceeded. We were just about to initial the agreement, and we consulted them, of course, about its content. Their spokesman said that while the agreement did not contain everything he would have liked, he and his colleagues could nevertheless recommend it to the people of Hong Kong in good conscience. In good conscience. That means a lot to us. If that is what the leaders of Hong Kong's own community believe, then we have truly fulfilled the heavy responsibility we feel for their long-term future. That agreement required imagination, skill, hard work and perseverence – in other words it required Geoffrey Howe.

In Europe, too, through firmness and determination, we have achieved a long-term settlement of Britain's budget contributions, a fair deal for Britain and for Europe too. If we had listened to the advice of other party leaders, Britain would not have done half as well. But patient diplomacy and occasionally, I confess, a little impatient diplomacy, did the trick.

We have also at last begun to curb surplus food production in the Community. We know that for some farmers this has meant a painful adjustment and we are very much aware of their difficulties. Their work and their success are the great strength to our country. Michael Jopling [Minister of Agriculture] and his colleagues will continue to fight to achieve a fair deal for them.

We have also won agreement on the need to keep the Community's spending under proper control. The Community can now enter on a new chapter and use its energies and influence to play a greater part in world affairs, as an example of what democracies can accomplish, as a very powerful trading group and as a strong force for freedom.

We had one of the most interesting debates of this conference on unemployment, which we all agree is the scourge of our times. To have over three million people unemployed in this country is bad enough, even though we share this tragic problem with other nations. But to suggest, as some of our opponents have, that we do not care about it is as deeply wounding as it is utterly false.

Do they really think that we do not understand what it means for the family man who cannot find a job, who has to sit at home with a sense of failure and despair? Or that we do not understand how hopeless the world must seem to a young person who has not yet succeeded in getting his first job? Of course we know; of course we see, and of course we care. However could they say that we welcome unemployment as a political weapon?

What better news could there be for any Government than the news that unemployment is falling? The day cannot come too soon for me. Others, while not questioning our sincerity, argue that our policies will not achieve our objectives. They look back forty years, to the post-war period, when we were poised to launch a brave new world, a time when we all thought we had the cure to unemployment.

In that confident dawn it seemed that having won the war, we knew how to win the peace. Keynes had provided the diagnosis. It was all set out in the 1944 White Paper on unemployment. I bought it then, I have it still. My name is on the top of it 'Margaret H. Roberts'.

One of my staff took one look at it and said, 'Good heavens, I didn't know it was as old as that'. We all read that White Paper very carefully, but the truth was that some politicians took some part of the formula in it and conveniently ignored the rest. I re-read it frequently.

Those politicians overlooked the warning in that paper that Government action must not weaken personal enterprise or exonerate the citizen from the duty of fending for himself. They disregarded the advice that wages must be related to productivity and, above all, they neglected the warning that without a rising standard of industrial efficiency you cannot achieve a high level of employment combined with a rising standard of living.

Having ignored so much of that, and having ignored other parts of the formula for so much of the time, the result was that we ended up with high inflation and high unemployment. Now, this Government are heeding the warnings. They have acted on the basic truths that were set out all those years ago in that famous White Paper.

If I had come out with all this today some people would call it Thatcherite, but in fact it was vintage Maynard Keynes. He had a horror of inflation, a fear of too much state control and a belief in the market. We are heeding those warnings. We are taking the policy as a whole and not only in selected parts. We have already brought inflation down below 5 per cent. Output has been rising steadily since 1981 and investment is up substantially.

But if things are improving, why, you will ask, does unemployment not fall? That was the question one could feel throughout that debate, even though people know that there is always a time lag between getting the other things right and having a fall in unemployment. Why does unemployment not fall?

May I try to answer that question? First, more jobs are being created, as Tom King [then Employment Secretary] pointed out. Over the last year more than a quarter of a million extra jobs have been created, but the population of working age is also rising very fast, as the baby boom of the 1960s become the school-leavers of the 1980s. So, although the number of jobs are rising, the population of working age is also rising. And among the population of working age a larger proportion of married women are seeking work.

So you will see why we need more jobs just to stop unemployment rising and even more jobs to get it falling. On top of that, new technology has caused redundancy in many factories. But it has also created whole new industries providing products and jobs that only a few years ago were undreamed of. So it has two effects. The first one is redundancies; the second, and slightly later, new jobs as new products become possible. This has happened in history before. A few days ago I visited York, where I saw the first railway engine, Stephenson's Rocket. I thought of the jobs, the prospects and the hope that the new steam engines and the railways then brought to many people.

Communities queued up to be on a railway line, to have their own station. Those communities welcomed change and it brought them more jobs. I confess, I am very glad we have got the railways. If we were trying to build those same railways today I wonder whether we would ever get planning permission, it sometimes takes so long. That is one thing that can sometimes delay the coming into existence of jobs.

That was one example from history, but let us go through my lifetime, as we had this same phenomenon – redundancies from new technology, more jobs from new technology. In the 1940s, when I took a science degree, the new emerging industries were plastics, man-made fibres and television. Later it will be satellites, computers and telecommunications. Now it is biotechnology and information technology. Today our universities and science parks are identifying the needs of tomorrow. So, there are new industries and new jobs in the pipeline.

I remember an industrialist telling me when I first went into business, and I have always remembered it, 'Our job is to discover what the customer will buy and to produce it'. And in Wrexham the other day, at a youth training centre, I was delighted to see a poster saying 'It is the customer that makes pay days possible'. So these young people were not only learning new technology, they were learning the facts of business life and how we create new jobs.

It is the spirit of enterprise that provides new jobs; it is being prepared to venture and build a business. And the role of Government in helping to do that? It is in cutting taxes, cutting inflation, keeping costs down, cutting through regulations and removing obstacles to the growth of small businesses, for that is where many of the new jobs will come from – small businesses. The role of Government is also in providing better education and training.

The youth training scheme, now in its second year, was set up to give young people the necessary skills for the new technologies and the necessary approach to industry. A majority of the first year's graduates are getting jobs. A much bigger proportion of those leaving the youth training scheme are getting jobs, compared with those leaving the youth opportunities scheme. And so they should, because it is a much better training scheme and it will improve again this year.

I was very interested in it. David Young [as head of the Manpower Services Commission] started it, and I offered to take a trainee for our office, No. 10 Downing Street. We would love to have one. He or she might not have made it to be Prime Minister in one year, but the work at No. 10, because we have a staff of about 100 to run the office, is varied and interesting and we really wanted to take on a trainee. We also said that we would take some trainees into the other parts of the civil service.

At first the unions said yes; then they said no. And the result is that young people have been denied training places. The same problem arose at Jaguar. First the unions said yes; then they said no. So 130 unemployed teenagers have been denied training. That means young people were denied jobs. We cannot create jobs without the willing co-operation not only of employers but of trade unions and all the work force in industry and commerce.

Yesterday, in the debate, we were urged to spend more money on capital investment. It looks a very attractive idea, but to spend more in one area means spending less in another, or it means putting up taxes. In Government we are constantly faced with these difficult choices. If we want more for investment I have to ask my colleagues in Cabinet 'What are you going to give up? Or you? Or you? Or you? Or you?' Or should I perhaps ask them 'Whose pay claim are you going to cut? The doctors? The police? The nurses?' I do not find many takers, because we have honoured the reviews of pay for doctors, nurses and the police, and others in full.

You would not have cheered me if we had not done so and quite right, too. I am bringing this to you because although people can say that the way to solve unemployment is to give a higher capital allocation I have to ask 'What are we going to give up?' Or I have to turn to Nigel Lawson and ask him which taxes would he put up. Would it be income tax? Personal income tax is already too high. Value added tax? I should get a pretty frosty reception from Nigel and I should get a pretty frosty reception from you. But I would be loth to ask him, anyway. But, you see, Governments have to make these difficult choices, because as you know, whether you are running households or your own businesses, there is a certain amount of income and you are soon in trouble if you do not live within it.

What I want to say to you is that we do consider these difficult choices in the public expenditure annual round, and we are just coming up to it. And we have managed to allocate a very considerable sum to capital investment. Indeed we have found the money for the best investment projects on offer. Believe you me, it has been because of very good management in each and every Department; it has been cutting out waste so that we could make room for these things and be certain that we could say to you that we were getting value for money.

Let me give you a few examples of some of the investment projects for which we have found money by careful budgeting. There is the M25 road for example. It has been completed. British Railways has been given the green light to go ahead with electrification if it can make it pay. We have started or built forty-nine new hospitals since 1979. Capital investment in the nationalised industries as a whole is going up. Of course, we look at various things like new power stations, and in a year after drought we look at things like more investment in the water supply industry. So we are going ahead with major capital investment.

So what is the conclusion that we are coming to? It is that it is the spirit of enterprise that creates new jobs. And it is the Government's task to create the right framework, the right financial framework in which that can flourish, and to cut the obstacles which sometimes handicap the birth of enterprise. And also to manage our own resources carefully and well.

That is more or less what that employment policy White Paper in 1944 said. Let me just return to it. On page 1 it states 'For employment cannot be created by Act of Parliament or by Government action alone . . . the success of the policy outlined in this paper will ultimately depend on the understanding and support of the community as a whole – and especially on the efforts of employers and workers in industry'. It was true then. It is true now. And those are the policies that we are following and shall continue to follow, because those are the policies that we believe will ultimately create the genuine jobs for the future. In the meantime it is our job to try to mitigate the painful effects of change, and that we do, as you know, by generous redundancy payments and also by a community enterprise scheme which not only finds jobs for the long-term unemployed, but finds them in a way which brings great benefits to the communities. And then, of course, where there are redundancy schemes in steel, and now in coal, the industries themselves set up enterprise agencies both to give help to those who are made redundant and to provide new training. All of this is a highly constructive policy both for the creation of jobs and a policy to cushion the effects of change.

May I turn now to the coal industry. For a little over seven months we have been living through an agonising strike. Let me make it absolutely clear. The miners' strike was not of this Government's seeking, nor of its making. We have heard in debates at this conference some of the aspects that have made this dispute so repugnant to so many people. We were reminded by a colliery manager that the NUM always used to accept that a pit should close when the losses were too great to keep it open. And that the miners set great store by investment in new pits and new seams. Under this Government that new investment is happening in abundance. You can almost repeat the figures with me – £2 million in capital investment in the mines for every day this Government has been in power. So no shortage of capital investment.

We heard moving accounts from two working miners about just what they have to face as they try to make their way to work. The sheer bravery of those men and thousands like them who have kept the mining industry alive is beyond praise. 'Scabs' their former workmates call them. Scabs? They are lions. What a tragedy it is when miners attack their workmates. Not only are they members of the same union, but the working miner is saving both their futures because it is the working miners, whether in Nottinghamshire, Derbyshire, Lancashire, Leicestershire, Staffordshire, Warwickshire, North Wales or Scotland, it is the working miners who have kept faith with those who buy our coal and without whose custom thousands of jobs in the mining industry would be already lost.

Then we heard, unforgettably, from the incomparable Mrs Irene McGibbon who told us what it is like to be the wife of a working miner during this strike. She told us of the threats and intimidation suffered by herself and her family and even her 11-year-old son. But what she endured only stiffened her resolve. To face the picket line day after day must take a very special kind of courage, but it takes as much, perhaps even more, for the housewife who has to stay at home alone. Men and women like that are what we are proud to call the best of British. And our police who uphold the law with an independence and a restraint, perhaps only to be found in this country, are the admiration of the world.

To be sure, the miners had a good deal. To try to prevent a strike the National Coal Board gave the miners the best ever pay offer, the highest ever investment and, for the first time, the promise that no miner would lose his job against his will. This we did despite the fact that the bill for losses in the coal industry last year was bigger than the annual bill for all the doctors and dentists in all the National Health Service hospitals in the United Kingdom. Let me repeat it: the annual losses in the coal industry are enormous – £1.3 billion last year. You have to find that money as taxpayers. It is equal to the sum we pay in salaries to all the doctors and dentists in the National Health Service.

This is a dispute about the right to go to work of those who have been denied the right to go to vote. And we must never forget that the overwhelming majority of trade unionists, including many striking miners, deeply regret what has been done in the name of trade unionism. When this strike is over, and one day it will be, we must do everything we can to encourage moderate and responsible trade unionism so that it can once again take its respected and valuable place in our industrial life.

Meanwhile, we are faced with the present executive of the National

Union of Mineworkers. They know that what they are demanding has never been granted either to miners or to workers in any other industry. Why, then, demand it? Why ask for what they know cannot be conceded? There can be only one explanation. They did not want a settlement. They wanted a strike. Otherwise they would have ballotted on the coal board's offer. Indeed, one-third of the miners did have a ballot and voted overwhelmingly to accept the offer.

What we have seen in this country is the emergence of an organised revolutionary minority who are prepared to exploit industrial disputes, but whose real aim is the breakdown of law and order and the destruction of democratic parliamentary government. We have seen the same sort of thugs and bullies at Grunwick, more recently against Eddy Shah in Stockport, and now organised into flying squads around the country. If their tactics were to be allowed to succeed, if they are not brought under the control of the law, we shall see them again at every industrial dispute organised by militant union leaders anywhere in the country.

One of the speakers earlier in the conference realised this fact, realised that what they are saying is 'Give us what we want or we are prepared to go on with violence'. He referred to Danegeld. May I add to what that speaker said? 'We never pay anyone Danegeld, no matter how trifling the cost; for the end of that game is oppression and shame, and the nation that plays it is lost.' Yes, Rudyard Kipling. Who could have put it better? Democratic change there has always been in this, the home of democracy, but the sanction for change is the ballot box. It seems that there are some who are out to destroy any properly elected Government. They are out to bring down the framework of law. That is what we have seen in this strike. And what is the law they seek to defy? It is the common law created by fearless judges and passed down across the centuries. It is legislation scrutinised and enacted by the Parliament of a free people. It is legislation passed through a House of Commons, a Commons elected once every five years by secret ballot of one citizen, one vote. This is the way our law was fashioned, and that is why British justice is renowned across the world.

No Government owns the law. It is the law of the land, the heritage of the people. 'No man is above the law, and no man is below it; nor do we ask any man's permission when we require him to obey it. Obedience to the law is demanded as a right – not asked as a favour.' So said Theodore Roosevelt.

The battle to uphold the rule of law calls for the resolve and commitment of the British people. Our institutions of justice, the courts and the police require the unswerving support of every law-abiding citizen, and I believe that they will receive it.

The nation faces what is probably the most testing crisis of our time

– the battle between the extremists and the rest. We are fighting, as we have always fought, for the weak as well as for the strong. We are fighting for great and good causes. We are fighting to defend them against the power and might of those who rise up to challenge them. This Government will not weaken. This nation will meet that challenge. Democracy will prevail.

CONSERVATIVE
PARTY CONFERENCE

* BLACKPOOL *

11th October 1985

MY FIRST WORDS must be of gratitude to those who organised this conference and looked after our security, bringing us safely to this great meeting.

There are many here today who still bear the scars of injury and bereavement inflicted last year by terrorists when they struck in the hours of darkness. It reminds us of the risks we all take, and will continue to take, for freedom.

I should like, too, to say a word about our friend and colleague John Gummer, whose dedication and tirelessness in those traumatic hours and for many days afterwards, won universal admiration. We thank him for his Chairmanship of our Party, for his unfailing sense of duty and loyalty, and wish him well in his new work as a member of our ministerial team.

Nobody could have followed this conference, or listened to the speeches made here this week, without being struck by one overriding impression. It has been a serious, friendly and responsible conference, a conference of those who know what it means for a political party to hold office, a conference of those who understand the realities of power exercised responsibly, the limitations, the dilemmas and the agonised choices which face those in Government.

Not for us the partisan rhetoric of class warfare, uttered with clenched fists through clenched lips. Not for us the bland blueprints of those who have never sweated on the actual building site of responsible office, nor ever will. For us the keynote has been idealism tempered by realism, and I am sure you have been very impressed by the quality and confidence of our whole team of Ministers.

For my part, I would like to add my congratulations and thanks to all those who have taken the chair at this conference with skill and unfailing good humour. In our Party we really rather like one another.

It is ten years since I first addressed this conference as Leader, in the same town – we all love Blackpool – in the same hall and on this same platform. I remember that meeting as though it were yesterday: the welcome, the warmth, the generous support that came from the hall. I already knew only too well the task that faced me, but I had not fully realised the strength that would be given to me by our people and was to sustain me first in the years of Opposition and then as Prime Minister.

In that speech I said that it was not part of my purpose to preside over the continuing decline of Britain, over diminishing international esteem, or over the ebb of our independent spirit. I also said it was not part of my policy to perpetuate Socialism by proxy.

Do you remember the Labour Britain of 1979? It was a Britain in which union leaders held their members and our country to ransom; a Britain that still went to international conferences but was no longer taken seriously; a Britain that was known as the sick man of Europe and which spoke the language of compassion but which suffered the winter of discontent. Governments had failed to tackle the real problems. They dodged difficult problems rather than face up to them. The question they asked was not 'will the medicine work?' but 'will it taste all right?'

When we Conservatives said 'this is the way', they said 'forget it'. We were told 'you can't reform trade union leaders; you can't reform trade unions, their leaders won't let you'. But we did. We were told 'you can't abolish price and wage controls; inflation will go up'. But we did, and it came down. We were told 'you can't give council tenants the right to buy'. But we did and the houses sold like hot cakes. They said 'you can't denationalise; the unions won't wear it'. But we did, and the work force positively snapped up the shares. And we were told 'you'll never stand a major industrial strike, let alone a coal strike'. It lasted a whole year but we did just that – and won.

It was a strike conducted with violence and intimidation on the picket line and in the villages. Yet Labour supported that strike to the bitter end. Indeed, three months into the strike Mr Kinnock told Mr Scargill publicly that there was 'no alternative but to fight – all other roads are shut off.' What do you think would have happened if Mr Scargill had won? I think the whole country knows the answer – Neil would have knelt. Courage is not making a speech in Bournemouth long after the event. Courage is what you show in the heat of battle, not at the post-mortem.

Real courage was the courage shown by the working miners, by the working lorry drivers, by the working railwaymen, by the working steelmen, by the working dockers – the very people the Labour Party disowned. But we Conservatives stood with them, the nation stood with us, and a major strike, called without a ballot of its members, failed. It was a notable victory for a free law-abiding people and their freely elected democratic Government.

In the six and a half years we have served the nation much has been achieved. It has been said at this conference many times but let me repeat it. The nation's output, the nation's investment, the nation's standard of living are at an all-time high. Inflation is down, and this morning we heard that it had gone down further. Personal ownership is growing. Our overseas assets have multiplied more than sixfold in six years. They now bring us an annual income of some £3,000 million a year. There are 700 additional new businesses starting up every week. Indeed, for the first time in our history the number of companies in Britain has topped one million.

Rates of income tax are down. Three major taxes have been abolished. And on Wednesday you heard my next door neighbour, the Chancellor of the Exchequer, in confident mood. On the social services, you have heard me say that the Health Service was safe with us. So it was, so it is, and so it will be.

But our opponents have conducted a relentless campaign to convey the opposite. The only way to nail a lie constantly repeated is to repeat the truth even more frequently. We have more doctors and nurses and they are treating more patients than ever. And it took a Conservative Government to give the nurses the independent Pay Review Body for which they were asking. The Royal College of Nursing had said consistently over the years: 'Our nurses never strike. The patient comes first.'

Pensioners, too, have been the object of a sustained and particularly cruel campaign of false propaganda. Let me say this to every pensioner. The basic pension goes on. That was never in doubt. And if anyone tells you otherwise don't believe them. Under this Conservative Government the pension has been increased by more than prices. And when it goes up again next month, it will be worth even more than ever before. All this is a remarkable record of which every Conservative can be proud. But there is much more to do.

I am only too painfully aware of the problem of unemployment. It affects not only Britain but the whole of Europe. But that does nothing to relieve the anxiety and frustration of someone who can't find a job. People say 'You do understand?' 'Of course, I do.' There is no problem which occupies more of my thinking and that of my colleagues. Scarcely a day passes without the Government looking at new ways of speeding job creation. People say 'make it easier for firms to take on more employees'. We have done. We've abolished Labour's tax on jobs and this week we cut National Insurance contributions for the lower paid. They say: 'Help people to start up in businesses on their own'. We're doing that by the highly successful enterprise allowance, and by cutting red tape, though heaven knows there's plenty still to be cut. They say: 'Train more young people'. We are, with the largest youth training programme this country has ever seen. The millionth young person will join before Christmas. That is a great achievement. I have seen it at work myself – in Glasgow and Chester, in Wrexham and Surrey, in Cornwall and all over the country. Young people working hard and well, many of them taken on later by the employer who has trained them. And we are expanding this programme so that everyone under the age of 18 can have either a job or education or training, and unemployment will not be an option.

People say, too – we heard it again at the conference; so many of these things we have heard here – 'Give the unemployed the chance to work for the community'. Right. We have expanded the community programme to 230,000 people next year. Then they say: 'Let more people retire early'. Many companies are doing just that, and the Government have special schemes which enable some to retire to make way for others looking for work.

We are doing all these things, and a lot more beside, but I will not list them all. But there is one thing we will not do. We will not reflate. We are sometimes told by politicians and pollsters that people would prefer more inflation and less unemployment. You cannot choose to have either inflation or unemployment. They are not alternatives. Past Governments have tried that. They have deliberately created inflation in the hope of reducing unemployment. It always finished up with worse inflation and worse unemployment. You cannot build a secure future on dishonest money.

There is a fundamental truth from which no Government can escape. It is customers who create business, and it is business which creates jobs. And it is happening. In the last two years some 650,000 additional jobs have been created, more than in the rest of the European Community put together. The jobs are coming and enterprise is returning to Britain. That is where the new jobs will come from.

I share the deep concern of parents about the education of our children. The basic teaching you receive in school can influence the rest of your life and shape your whole future. Today, more money is being spent per pupil than ever before. There are more teachers proportionately to pupils than ever before. Their training is better than ever before. But, alas, that has not solved all the difficulties.

We are all worried about the teachers' strike and its effect on the children. The burden on heads and deputy heads is enormous, and we are very much aware of the strains on them and on many teachers. So, some £1,250 million of your money has therefore been pledged in pay for teachers, over and above the annual increases. That would mean pay scales in November next year running from £7,500 a year for a new graduate to more than £24,000 for the head of a big secondary school, with much better promotion opportunities in between. By the way, I notice that the Labour Opposition regard £20,000 a year as their definition of the rich to be soaked by higher taxes. I do not agree, and I do not suppose that those head teachers do either.

We believe that this offer would not only be a fair deal for teachers but it would enable us, first, to have a salary system which would reward the better teachers, and, second, to spell out teachers' duties clearly so that we can get rid of all the arguments. I most earnestly hope that this strike will soon be settled. Teachers should lead by example, and this is a bad one.

While many parents are well content with the education their children are receiving, the story for some, especially in the inner city areas, is very different: poor examination results; lack of good discipline; the unhappiness which some quiet and sensitive children sometimes suffer; political indoctrination in our schools; and the attempts by some local education authorities to control the curriculum and use it for political ends. No wonder parents are worried, and so are a lot of the teachers, especially those who have to deal with disruptive pupils who make their task difficult and exhausting. What is more, when teachers take disciplinary measures they do not always receive the backing from the local education authority which they are entitled to expect. Some teachers and parents are speaking out: those who believe, as we do, that the schools of this country are for teaching and learning and not for political indoctrination. In the debate we had you pulled no punches. I prefer it that way. I believe that you performed a public service by bringing this matter into the open, and Sir Keith [Joseph] and his colleagues will do everything in their power to root out this pernicious influence and to see that our children have the education to which they are entitled.

Last week, at his party conference, the Labour leader gave what we were told was a clarion call to moderation in the Labour Party. It was, announced Labour's deputy leader – now there is an unbiased observer – a turning point in history. But 'by their fruits ye shall know them'. So never mind the PR, let us have a look at the policies.

Last week at Bournemouth the Labour Party voted to scrap the laws which give union members a secret ballot and to hand back to the leaders, those barons of the block vote, their former feudal powers. They voted to give up the British independent nuclear deterrent for nothing in return. They voted to take political control over the operations of the police. They voted to indemnify councils and trade unions who choose to break the law for political ends. Anything else? I have hardly started.

Here are some Labour policies for the next general election in two or three years' time. They would nationalise and renationalise our industry with scant regard for the newly acquired shares of employees. There would be no automatic right to buy your own council house. Decisions would be left to Labour councils such as Sheffield,

Hackney and Camden, and you can imagine what sort of a deal you would get from them.

Labour would also hijack and direct the pension and insurance fund money of some twelve million people. Independent schools would go, and quickly. There would be the usual mishmash of higher taxes and, I need hardly say, higher borrowing. 'To borrow and to borrow and to borrow' is not Macbeth with a heavy cold. It is Labour Party policy. But most people do not want to mortgage the future and leave their children to pick up the bill.

Labour's banner reads back, back to a high tax society. Back to the old days of inflation by social contract. Back to rule by Congress House, when the Labour Party was a wholly owned subsidiary of the unions.

The Labour Party is two different factions in a state of civil war, with the Left steadily gaining ground. As the old stagers retire or are forced out they are replaced by the new militant Left. You can see Socialism in action today in the council chambers of local government in Liverpool, Lambeth, Haringey and many others, so vividly described at this conference. That is what it would be like if Labour ever got power at Westminster. The militant Left will not be beaten by brave words and ritual disclaimers. If the Labour leadership is genuinely against these people why do they not expel them? Is not the real reason that they are a bigger and bigger part of the Labour Party and that the present leadership cannot do without them?

And where do the so-called Alliance stand? Take defence. Did we see them reaffirm one-sided disarmament or did they decide this year to keep a few missiles? Or is it only the ones that are out of date they would keep? Or is it a case of defending all of the people some of the time or some of the people all of the time? It is all very confusing.

Those who want the country to have a strong and sure defence can't rely on the Labour Party, the SDP or the Liberals. They can rely on us. By the end of this century it is predicted that several more countries will have acquired nuclear weapons. Labour wants Britain to give them up. At the very time when any sensible person would be renewing his insurance cover, Labour wants to cancel Britain's policy altogether. Moreover, they want to get rid of American bases from Britain and all nuclear weapons from British soil.

Does anyone who has witnessed Mr Gorbachev's performance think that he respects weakness? No, it is recognition of the West's strength and cohesion that has brought the Soviet Union back to the negotiating table. Our wish is to see substantial reductions in nuclear weapons, provided they are balanced and verifiable. I know that will be President's Reagan's objective at his meeting with Mr Gorbachev, and he has our full support and good wishes as he goes to Geneva. The West could have no better or braver champion.

The whole country is rightly concerned about security at home, about violence in the streets. We utterly condemn anyone and everyone who takes part in riots in Britain. Whoever these people are who riot, burn and murder; whoever they are organised by, there is no excuse, no justification whatsoever, for such crime and vandalism. Those who take to the streets on the first available pretext, to fire, loot and plunder, will be subject to the full rigours of the criminal law.

In Tottenham and Handsworth the police suffered a hail of bricks and petrol bombs, apparently ready to hand. Yet one of the delegates to the Labour Party conference was loudly applauded when he called the police 'The Enemy'. 'Enemy?' The overwhelming majority of the British people regard the police as friends: they admire and are deeply thankful for the courage of the police and the courage of their families.

It isn't the police who create threats to public order. All too often they are the victims, as we saw only too tragically at Tottenham. Nor is it social conditions that generate violence. Yes, unemployment breeds frustration, but it's an insult to the unemployed to suggest that a man who doesn't have a job is likely to break the law.

In the 1930s, when unemployment was proportionately higher, and virtually unrelieved by benefits, crime levels were not higher, they were lower. In parts of the world where the standard of living is high, the environment attractive, and jobs are relatively plentiful – parts of America for example – crime is worse than in Britain. In a free country everyone has to choose. And the overwhelming majority of our fellow citizens – black or white, in or out of work, living in the suburbs or city centres – freely make their choice. They respect the law; and they will have no truck with crime masquerading as social protest. The Government will continue steadfastly to back the police. If they need more men, more equipment, different equipment, they shall have them. We don't economise on protecting life and property. We shall oppose politicians, national or local, who want to interfere in the operational independence of the police. There is no place for politics in policing. But our concern about violence goes far beyond the riots.

A child abused, perhaps destroyed, within her own home can't begin to know where, if anywhere, to look for safety. An elderly couple, nervous to step outside their home, shouldn't have to look about them in fear. A teenager who's slid towards drugs may no longer be able to help himself. Who is to answer the child crying for help? Who is to protect the elderly couple? Who can win back the youngster hooked on drugs? Police, social workers, the voluntary organisations all must, and do, respond, but that's not enough. We are the neighbours of that child, of that elderly couple, of that youngster. Upholding the law can't be left to the police and the courts alone. We are all involved. We cannot pass by on the other side.

Government apart, the strengths of a civilised nation depend on the natural authority of the family, the school, the church and our great institutions. It is when that authority weakens – and it has weakened – that nations turn to the power of the State. When the power of the State increases, the dignity of the individual declines. Our national character and greatness was not founded on the all-embracing power of government. It was not founded on material worth. It was founded on freedom, orderly freedom, within the law. For without law, there can be no freedom.

In Britain today we have seen the hard Left operating within our political system, conspiring through union power or local government to break, defy and subvert the law. Because the Labour Party will not expel these people, a unique responsibility is placed on today's Conservative Party and Government. We have to conserve the rule of law itself, conserve it for people of all parties and of none.

That is our overriding duty. Success will require the co-operation of every law-abiding citizen. No one can opt out. Come with us, then, towards the next decade. Let us together set our sights on a Britain where three out of four families own their home, where owning shares is as common as having a car, where families have a degree of independence their forefathers could only dream about; a Britain where there is a resurgence of enterprise, with more people self-employed, more businesses and, therefore, more jobs; a Britain where there is a standard of health care far better than anything we have ever known, where savings keep their value and where people can look forward to their retirement, certain of their pension and confident of its buying power; a Britain where standards in our schools are a source of pride and where law-abiding men and women go their way in tranquillity with their children, knowing that their neighbourhood is safe and their country secure.

Step by step we are rolling back the frontiers of Socialism and returning power to the people. Yes, we have set our sights high. But these goals are within our reach. Let us ensure that we bring them within our grasp.

12

CONSERVATIVE PARTY CONFERENCE

* BOURNEMOUTH *

10th October 1986

THIS WEEK AT BOURNEMOUTH, we've had a most responsible conference: the conference of a Party which was the last Government, is the present Government, and will be the next Government. And we've heard from Ministers a series of forward-looking policies which are shaping the future of our country, and not only from Ministers, but from the body of the hall has come speech after speech of advice, encouragement and commitment. We are a Party which knows what it stands for and what it seeks to achieve. We are a Party which honours the past that we may build for the future.

Last week, at Blackpool, the Labour Party made the bogus claim that it was 'putting people first'.

Putting people first? Last week Labour voted to remove the right to a secret ballot before a strike, voted to remove the precious right we gave to trade union members to take their union to a court of law.

Putting people first? Last week Labour voted for the State to renationalise British Telecom and British Gas, regardless of the millions of people who have been able to own shares for the first time in their lives.

Putting people first? They voted to stop the existing right to buy council houses, a policy which would kill the hopes and dreams of so many families.

Labour may say they put people first: but, their conference voted to put Government first and that means putting people last. What the Labour Party of today wants is: housing municipalised, industry nationalised, the police service politicised, the judiciary radicalised, union membership tyrannised, and above all, the most serious of all, our defences neutralised. Never!

We have two other oppositions who have recently held their conferences, the Liberals and the SDP. Where they're not divided they're vague, and where they're not vague they're divided. At the moment they appear to be engaged in a confused squabble about whether or not Polaris should be abandoned or replaced, or renewed or re-examined. And if so, when; and how; and possibly why? If they can't agree on the defence of our country, they can't agree on anything. Where Labour has its Militant Tendency, they have their muddled tendency.

I'll have rather more to say about defence later. But just now I want to speak about Conservative policies, policies which spring from deeply held beliefs. The charge is sometimes made that our policies are only concerned with money and efficency. I am the first to acknowledge that morality is not, and never has been, the monopoly of any one Party. Nor do we claim that it is. But we do claim that it is the foundation of our policies.

Why are we Conservatives so opposed to inflation? Only because it puts up prices? No, because it destroys the value of people's savings. Because it destroys jobs, and with it people's hopes. That's what the fight against inflation is all about. Why have we limited the power of trade unions? Only to improve productivity? No, because trade union members want to be protected from intimidation and to go about their daily lives in peace – like everyone else in the land.

Why have we allowed people to buy shares in nationalised industries? Only to improve efficiency? No. To spread the nation's wealth among as many people as possible. And why are we setting up new kinds of schools in our towns and cities? To create privilege? No. To give families in some of our inner cities greater choice in the education of their children – a choice denied them by their Labour Councils. Enlarging choice is rooted in our Conservative tradition. And without choice, talk of morality is an idle and empty thing.

The theme of our conference this week is 'The Next Move Forward'. We have achieved a lot in seven short years. But there is still a great deal to be done for our country. The whole industrial world, not just Britain, is seeing change at a speed that our forebears never contemplated, much of it due to new technology. Old industries are declining. New ones are taking their place. Traditional jobs are being taken over by computers. People are choosing to spend their money in new ways. Leisure, pleasure, sport and travel: all these are big business today.

It would be foolish to pretend that this transition can be accomplished without problems. But it would be equally foolish to pretend that a country like Britain, which is so heavily dependent on trade with others, can somehow ignore what is happening in the rest of the world; can behave as if these great events have nothing to do with us; can resist change.

Yet that is exactly what Labour proposes to do: they want to put back the clock and set back the country. Back to State direction and control; back to the old levels of overmanning; back to the old inefficiencies; back to making life difficult for the very people on whom the future of Britain depends – the wealth creators, the scientists, the engineers, the designers, the managers, the inventors, all those on whom we rely to create the industries and jobs of the future.

What supreme folly. It defies all common sense – as do those Labour policies which, far from putting people first, would put them out of jobs. The prospects of young people would be blighted by Labour's minimum wage policy, because people could not then afford to employ them and give them a start in life. A quarter of a million jobs could be at risk. Many thousands of jobs would go from closing down American nuclear bases. And then Labour want sanctions against South Africa. Tens of thousands of people could lose their jobs in Britain – quite apart from the devastating consequences for black South Africans. Out would go jobs at existing nuclear power stations. Whatever happened to Harold Wilson's 'white heat of technological revolution'? On top of all this, jobs would also suffer as would-be investors in Britain took one look at Labour and decided to set up elsewhere. Labour say they would create jobs. But those policies would destroy jobs.

This Government has created the climate that's produced a million extra jobs over the past three years. Here in Britain, it is encouraging that more of the population are in work than in Italy, or France, or even Germany. Nevertheless, as you heard yesterday, more has to be done, and is being done. Meanwhile, no other country in Europe can rival our present range of help for people to train, and retrain and find jobs. Training is not a palliative for unemployment. Training will play an ever larger part in our whole industrial life. For only modern, efficient industry and commerce will produce the jobs our people need.

Our opponents would have us believe that all problems can be solved by State intervention. But Governments should not run business. Indeed, the weakness of the case for State ownership has become all too apparent. For State planners do not have to suffer the consequences of their mistakes. It's the taxpayers who have to pick up the bill.

This Government has rolled back the frontiers of the State, and will roll them back still further. So popular is our policy that it's being taken up all over the world. From France to the Philippines, from Jamaica to Japan, from Malaysia to Mexico, from Sri Lanka to Singapore, privatisation is on the move. There's even a special oriental version in China. The policies we have pioneered are catching on in country after country. We Conservatives believe in popular capitalism – believe in a property-owning democracy. And it works!

In Scotland recently, I was present at the sale of the millionth council house: to a lovely family with two children who can at last call their home their own. Now let's go for the second million! And what's more, millions have already become shareholders. And soon there will be opportunities for millions more, in British Gas, British Airways, British Airports and Rolls Royce. Who says we've run out of steam? We're in our prime! The great political reform of the last century was to enable more and more people to have a vote. Now the great Tory reform of this century is to enable more and more people to own property. Popular capitalism is nothing less than a crusade to enfranchise the many in the economic life of the nation. We Conservatives are returning power to the people. That is the way to one nation, one people.

You may have noticed there are many people who just can't bear good news. It's a sort of infection of the spirit and there's a lot of it about. In the eyes of these hand-wringing merchants of gloom and despondency, everything that Britain does is wrong. Any set-back, however small, any little difficulty, however local, is seen as incontrovertible proof that the situation is hopeless. Their favourite word is 'crisis'. It's a crisis when the price of oil goes up and a crisis when the price of oil comes down. It's a crisis if you don't build new roads, it's a crisis when you do. It's a crisis if Nissan does not come here, and it's a crisis when it does. It's being so cheerful that keeps them going.

What a rotten time these people must have, running round running everything down. Especially when there's so much to be proud of: inflation at its lowest level for twenty years; the basic rate of tax at its lowest level for forty years; the number of strikes at their lowest level for fifty years; the great advances in science and industry; the achievement of millions of our people in creating new enterprises and new jobs; the outstanding performance of the arts and music and entertainment worlds; and the triumphs of our sportsmen and women. They all do Britain proud. And we are mighty proud of them.

Our opponents, having lost the political argument, try another tack! They try to convey the impression that we don't care. So let's take a close look at those who make this charge. They're the ones who supported and maintained Mr Scargill's coal strike for a whole year, hoping to deprive industry, homes and pensioners of power, heat and light. They're the ones who supported the strike in the Health Service which lengthened the waiting time for operations, just when we were getting it down. They're the ones who supported the teachers' dispute which disrupted our children's education. They are those Labour Councillors who constantly accuse the police of provocation when they deal with violent crime and drugs in the worst areas of our inner cities. We're not going to take any lessons in caring from people with that sort of record.

We care profoundly about the rights of people to be protected against crime, hooliganism and the evil of drugs. The mugger, the rapist, the drug trafficker, the terrorist: all must suffer the full rigour of the law. And that's why this Party and this Government consistently back the police and the courts of law, in Britain and Northern Ireland. For without the rule of law, there can be no liberty.

It's because we care deeply about the Health Service, that we've launched the biggest hospital building programme in this country's history. Statistics tell only part of the story. But this Government is devoting more resources of all kinds to the Health Service than any previous Government. Over the past year or so, I've visited five hospitals. In the North West, at Barrow-in-Furness – I visited the first new hospital in that district since the creation of the Health Service forty years ago. In the North East – another splendid new hospital, at North Tyneside, with the most wonderful maternity unit and children's wards. Just north of London I went round St Albans' Hospital where new wards have been opened and new buildings are under way.

I visited the famous Elizabeth Garrett Anderson Hospital for Women, which this Government saved. And the service it provides is very special and greatly appreciated. Then, last week, I went back to the Royal Sussex County Hospital in Brighton, to open the new renal unit. Many of us have cause to be very thankful for that Brighton hospital. Everywhere patients were loud in their praise of the treatment they received from doctors and nurses whose devotion and skill we all admire.

This Government's record on the Health Service is a fine one. We're proud of it and we must see to it that people know how much we've done. Of course there are problems still to be solved. The fact that there's no waiting list in one area does not help you if you have to wait for an operation in your area. It doesn't help if there's a new hospital going up somewhere else, but not where you'd really like it. We are tackling these problems. And we shall go on doing so, because our commitment to the National Health Service is second to none. We've made great progress already. The debate we had on Wednesday, with its telling contributions from nurses and doctors in the Health Service, was enormously helpful to us. It's our purpose to work together and to continue steadily to improve the services that are provided in hospital and community alike. This is Conservatives putting care into action.

We care deeply that retired people should never again see their hard-earned savings decimated by runaway inflation. For example, take the pensioner who retired in 1963 with a thousand pounds of savings. Twenty years later, in 1983, it was only worth one hundred and sixty pounds. That is why we will never relent in the battle against inflation. It has to be fought and won every year.

We care passionately about the education of our children. Time and again we hear three basic messages: bring back the three Rs into our schools; bring back relevance into the curriculum; and bring back discipline into our classrooms. The fact is that education at all levels – teachers, training colleges, administrators – has been infiltrated by a permissive philosophy of self-expression. And we are now reaping the consequences which, for some children, have been disastrous.

Money by itself will not solve this problem. Money will not raise standards. But, by giving parents greater freedom to choose; by allowing head teachers greater control in their schools; by laying down national standards of syllabus and attainment, I am confident that we can really improve the quality of education – not just in the twenty new schools which were announced at this conference, but in every school in the land. And we'll back every teacher, head teacher and administrator who shares these ideals.

We care most of all about our country's security. The defence of the realm transcends all other issues. It is the foremost responsibility of any Government and any Prime Minister. For forty years, every Government of this country of every political persuasion has understood the need for strong defences by maintaining and modernising Britain's independent nuclear deterrent; by membership of the NATO Alliance, an alliance based on nuclear deterrence; and by accepting, and bearing in full, the obligations which membership brings. All this was common ground.

Last week, the Labour Party abandoned that ground. In a decision of the utmost gravity, Labour voted to give up Britain's independent nuclear deterrent unilaterally. Labour would also require the United States to remove its nuclear weapons from our soil and to close down its nuclear bases – weapons and bases which are vital, not only for Britain's defence, but for the defence of the entire Atlantic Alliance. Furthermore, Labour would remove Britain altogether from the protection of America's nuclear umbrella, leaving us totally unable to deter a nuclear attack. For you cannot deter, with conventional weapons, an enemy which has, and could threaten to use, nuclear weapons. Exposed to the threat of nuclear blackmail, there would be no option but to surrender.

Labour's defence policy – though 'defence' is scarcely the word – is an absolute break with the defence policy of every British Government since the Second World War. Let there be no doubt about the gravity of that decision. You cannot be a loyal member of NATO while disavowing its fundamental strategy. A Labour Britain would be a neutralist Britain. It would be the greatest gain for the Soviet Union in forty years. And they would have got it without firing a shot.

I believe that this total reversal of Labour's policy for the defence of our country will have come as a shock to many of Labour's traditional supporters. It was Labour's Nye Bevan who warned his Party against going naked into the conference chamber. It was Labour's Hugh Gaitskell who promised the country to fight, and fight and fight again against the unilateral disarmers in his own party. That fight was continued by his successors. Today the fight is over, because the present leadership are the unilateral disarmers. The Labour Party of Attlee, of Gaitskell, of Wilson is dead. And no one has more surely killed it than the present leader of the Labour Party.

There are some policies which can be reversed. But weapon development and production takes years and years. Moreover, by repudiating NATO's nuclear strategy, Labour would fatally weaken the Atlantic Alliance and the United States' commitment to Europe's defence. The damage caused by Labour's policies would be irrevocable. Not only present but future generations would be at risk.

Of course there are fears about the terrible destructive power of nuclear weapons. But it is the balance of nuclear forces that has preserved peace for forty years in a Europe which twice in the previous thirty years tore itself to pieces. The nuclear balance has preserved peace not only from nuclear war but from conventional war in Europe as well. And it has saved the young people of two generations from being called up to fight as their parents and grandparents were. As Prime Minister, I could not remove that protection from the lives of present and future generations.

Let every nation know that Conservative Governments, now and in the future, will keep Britain's obligations to its allies. The freedom of all its citizens and the good name of our country depend upon it.

This weekend President Reagan and Mr Gorbachev are meeting in Reykjavik. Does anyone imagine that Mr Gorbachev would be prepared to talk at all if the West had already disarmed? It is the strength and unity of the West which has brought the Russians to the negotiating table. The policy of Her Majesty's Opposition is a policy that would help our enemies and harm our friends. I believe it totally misjudges the character of the British people. After the Liberal Party conference, after the SDP conference, after the Labour conference, there is now only one party in this country with an effective policy for the defence of the realm and that party is the Conservative Party.

Throughout this conference we've heard of the great achievements of the last seven years. Their very success now makes possible the next moves forward which have been set out this week. And we shall complete the manifesto for the next Election within the next eighteen months. That manifesto will be a programme for further bold and radical steps in keeping with our most deeply held beliefs. For we do our best for our country when we are true to our convictions.

As we look forward to the next century, we have a vision of the society we wish to see – the vision we all serve. We want to see a Britain where there is an ever-widening spread of ownership, with the independence and dignity it brings – a Britain which takes care of the weak in their time of need. We want to see a Britain where the spirit of enterprise is strong enough to conquer unemployment north and south – a Britain in which the attitude of 'them and us' has disappeared from our lives. We want to see a Britain whose schools are a source of pride and where education brings out the best in every child – a Britain where excellence and effort are valued and honoured. We want to see a Britain where our streets are free from fear, day and night.

Above all, we want to see a Britain which is respected and trusted in the world, which values the great benefits of living in a free society, and is determined to defend them. Our duty is to safeguard our country's interests, and to be reliable friends and allies. The failure of the other parties to measure up to what is needed, places an awesome responsibility upon us. I believe that we have an historic duty to discharge that responsibility and to carry into the future all that is best and unique in Britain. I believe that our Party is uniquely equipped to do it.

I believe the interests of Britain can now only be served by a third Conservative victory.

```
CONSERVATIVE
PARTY CONFERENCE

* BLACKPOOL *

9th October 1987
```

IT IS MY FIRST DUTY and pleasure to pay tribute to the police, and especially to the Lancashire police for the protection they have given to our conference at Blackpool. Their professionalism, their dedication have ensured that, no matter what the threat, nothing will stop the free debate of a political party in Britain. The police and the security forces are the true guardians of our liberties, and to them we extend our deep gratitude.

A lot has happened since we last met. There was, for instance, our election victory in June. They tell me that makes it three wins in a row. Just like Lord Liverpool. And he was Prime Minister for fifteen years. It's rather encouraging.

It was an historic victory. And I want to thank all those who did so much. Above all, our Chairman, Norman Tebbit. Norman and Margaret hold, and will always hold, a unique place in our esteem and affection. Thank you, too, Margaret.

On the 11th June, we even won some nine seats we failed to gain in 1983. And we won back three we lost at by-elections. To the victors we say – congratulations. To our former colleagues who lost – come back soon. We miss you.

Just why did we win? I think it is because we knew what we stood for. We said what we stood for; and we stuck by what we stood for. And since the election, it sometimes seems we are the only party that does.

Twelve years ago, I first stood on this platform as Leader of the Conservative Party. Now one or two things have changed since 1975. In that year we were still groaning under Labour's so-called 'social contract'. People said we should never be able to govern again. Remember how we had all been lectured about political impossibility? You couldn't be a Conservative, and sound like a Conservative, and win an election – they said. You certainly couldn't win an election and then act like a Conservative and win another election. And – this was absolutely beyond dispute – you couldn't win two elections and go on behaving like a Conservative, and yet win a third election. Don't you harbour just the faintest suspicion that somewhere along the line something went wrong with that theory?

Right up to 11th June, the Labour Party, the Liberals and the SDP were busy saying that Conservatism doesn't work. Oddly enough, since the 12th June, they've been saying that it does. So our political opponents are now feverishly packaging their policies to look like ours. It's interesting that no Party now dares to say openly that it will take away from the people what we have given back to the people.

Labour's language may alter, their presentation may be slicker, but underneath it's still the same old Socialism. Far be it from me to deride the sinner that repenteth. The trouble with Labour is they want the benefit of repentance without renouncing the original sin. No way!

And the so-called 'Alliance'? During the election campaign I used to wonder what the Alliance leaders meant by consensus politics. I have a feeling that, if Dr Owen didn't know it before, he knows now: six inches of fraternal steel beneath the shoulder blades.

We are a successful party leading a successful nation. I'm often asked what's the secret. It's really quite simple. What we have done is to re-establish at the heart of British politics a handful of simple truths.

First, no economy can thrive if Government debases the coinage. No society can be fair or stable when inflation eats up savings and devalues the pound in everyone's pocket. Inflation threatens democracy itself. We've always put its defeat at the top of our agenda. For it's a battle which never ends. It means keeping your budget on a sound financial footing. Not just one year, but every year and that's why we need Nigel Lawson.

Second, men and women need the incentive that comes from keeping more of what they earn. No one can say that people aren't interested in their take-home pay. If that were true, a lot of trade union leaders would be out of a job. So as economic growth has taken off, we've cut income tax. And as soon as we prudently can, we'll do it again.

Third, as people earn more, they want to own more. They value the security which comes from ownership – whether of shares or homes. Soon there will be more shareholders than trade unionists in this country. Of course, not all trade unionists are shareholders – yet. But I hope that before long they will be. Home ownership too has soared. And to extend the right to council tenants, we had to fight the battle as you know, the battle in Parliament, every inch of the way – against Labour opposition, and against Liberal opposition.

Does the Labour Leader now applaud what has happened? Does the Liberal Leader welcome it? Surely, now that it's proved so popular, it must be the sort of liberating measure of which even he would approve.

For years we Conservatives had talked about wanting to create a property-owning democracy. Looking back, I wonder whether we did as much as we should have done to achieve that goal. But I don't believe that anyone will be able, in the years ahead, to make a similar charge against this Government. Indeed, extending ownership has been one of the achievements of which I am most proud.

Fourth, it is our passionate belief that free enterprise and competition are the engines of prosperity and the guardians of liberty. These ideas have shaped free political institutions and brought unimagined wealth to countries and continents. Just look at what we have achieved – low inflation; tax cuts; wider ownership; a revival of enterprise and, over the last year, unemployment has fallen at record speed by 400,000. And we want it to fall further. With continued economic growth, it should.

Our economic success has enabled Britain to play a more prominent role in the world at large. We are now the second biggest investor in the world, and the very model of a stable economy. And that's why Nigel Lawson has been able to play a leading role in helping to tackle the world debt crisis. International bankers, the finance ministers of other nations: they all listen to you a lot harder when they owe you money rather than the other way round.

The old Britain of the 1970s, with its strikes, poor productivity, low investment, winters of discontent, above all its gloom, its pessimism, its sheer defeatism – that Britain is gone. We now have a new Britain, confident, optimistic, sure of its economic strength – a Britain to which foreigners come to admire, to invest, yes, and to imitate.

I have reminded you where the great political adventure began and where it has led. But is this where we pitch our tents? Is this where we dig in? Absolutely not. Our third election victory was only a staging post on a much longer journey. I know with every fibre of my being that it would be fatal for us just to stand where we are now. What would be our slogan for the 1990s if we did that? Would 'consolidate' be the word that we stitch on our banners? Whose blood would run faster at the prospect of five years of consolidation? Of course, we secure what we've achieved. But we move on – applying our principles and beliefs to even more challenging ground. For our purpose as Conservatives is to extend opportunity – and choice – to those who have so far been denied them.

Our most important task in this Parliament is to raise the quality of education. You heard what Kenneth Baker had to say about it in that most interesting, stimulating debate we had the other day. It's in the national interest. And it's in the individual interest of every parent and, above all, of every child. We want education to be part of the answer to Britain's problems, not part of the cause.

To compete successfully in tomorrow's world – against Japan,

Germany and the United States – we need well-educated, well-trained, creative young people. If education is backward today, national performance will be backward tomorrow.

It's the plight of individual boys and girls which worries me most. Too often, our children don't get the education they need – the education they deserve. In the inner cities – where youngsters must have a decent education if they are to have a better future – that opportunity is all too often snatched from them by hard-Left education authorities and extremist teachers. Children who need to be able to count and multiply are learning anti-racist mathematics – whatever that may be. Children who need to be able to express themselves in clear English are being taught political slogans. Children who need to be taught to respect traditional moral values are being taught that they have an inalienable right to be gay. And children who need encouragement – and children do so much need encouragement – they are being taught that our society offers them no future. All of those children are being cheated of a sound start in life – yes, cheated.

Of course – in the country as a whole – there are plenty of excellent teachers and successful schools. And in every good school, and every good teacher, is a reminder of what too many young people are denied.

I believe that government must take the primary responsibility for setting standards for the education of our children. And that's why we are establishing a national curriculum for basic subjects. It is vital that children master essential skills: reading, writing, spelling, grammar, arithmetic; and that they understand basic science and technology. And for good teachers this will provide a foundation on which they can build with their own creative skill and professionalism.

But the key to raising standards is to enlist the support of parents. The Labour Left – hard, soft and in-between – they hate the idea that people should be able to choose. In particular, they hate the idea that parents should be able to choose their children's education. The Conservative Party believes in parental choice. We are now about to take two dramatic steps forward in extending choice in education.

First, we will allow popular schools to take in as many children as space will permit. And this will stop local authorities from putting artificially low limits on entry to good schools.

Second, we will give parents and governors the right to take their children's school out of the hands of the local authority and into the hands of their own governing body. This will create a new kind of school funded by the State, alongside the present State schools and the independent private schools. These new schools will be independent State schools. They will bring a better education to many children because the school will be in the hands of those who care most for it and for its future. There's no reason at all why local authorities should have a monopoly of free education. What principle suggests that this is right? What recent experience or practice suggests it is even sensible?

In these ways, we are furthering our Conservative tradition of extending opportunity more widely. This policy will be of greatest advantage, not to those schools where the parents are already satisfied with their children's education, but to those schools where the parents are dissatisfied and believe that their children could do a lot better. Nowhere is this policy more needed than in what have come to be known as 'inner cities'. It will profit those people most.

The phrase 'inner cities' is a kind of convenient shorthand for a host of problems. Cities have risen and declined throughout history. They have risen by responding to the opportunities, the markets, the technologies of their day have offered. And they declined when they clung to old, outdated ways and new markets passed them by. That is what's happened to many of our great cities.

Their decline was sometimes aggravated by the worst form of post-war town planning – a sort of social vandalism, carried out with the best of intentions but the worst of results. All too often, the planners cut the heart out of our cities. They swept aside the familiar city centres that had grown up over the centuries. They replaced them with a wedge of tower blocks and linking expressways, interspersed with token patches of grass and a few windswept piazzas, where pedestrians fear to tread. The planners didn't think: 'Are we breaking the pattern of people's lives. Are we cutting them off from their friends, their neighbours?' They didn't wonder: 'Are we uprooting whole communities?' They didn't ask 'Can children still play safely in the street?'

They didn't consider any of these things. Nor did they consult the police about how to design an estate in which people could walk safe from muggers and vandals. They simply set the municipal bulldozer to work. What folly, what incredible folly. And the people who didn't fit into this urban Utopia? They dispatched them to outlying estates without a pub or corner shop or anywhere to go. The schemes won a number of architectural awards. But they were a nightmare for the people. They snuffed out any spark of local enterprise. And they made people entirely dependent on the local authorities and the services they chose to provide.

As if that were not enough, some of our cities have also been dominated by Labour councils implacably hostile to enterprise. So when industries left, they piled higher rates on those that remained. When old markets vanished, they sought not new markets but new subsidies. They capitalised not on their strengths, but on their weaknesses. In fact they accelerated decline. So dying industries, soulless planning, municipal Socialism – these deprived the people of the most precious things in life: hope, confidence and belief in themselves. And that sapping of the spirit is at the very heart of urban decay.

To give back heart to our cities we must give back hope to the people. And it's beginning to happen – because today Britain has a strong and growing economy. Oh yes, recovery has come faster in some parts of the country than others. But now it is taking root in our most depressed urban landscapes. We all applaud the organisation 'Business in the Community' – it is over 300 major firms that have come together to assist in reviving the urban communities from which so many of them sprang.

So many of the amenities of our towns and cities – the parks and public gardens, the libraries and art galleries, the churches and schools – they had their origin in the philanthropy of men who made good themselves, and they wanted to do good for others. That impulse – that sense of obligation to the wider community – it is that we must enlist today.

I've seen the start of recovery for myself: on Teesside, in Gateshead, in Wolverhampton and the West Midlands. And in Glasgow, which is undergoing a remarkable revival, thanks largely to the work of George Younger and Malcolm Rifkind. I shall never forget one Glaswegian I met on my visit there. How do you do, I said. My name's Margaret Thatcher. Mine's Winston Churchill, he replied. And astonishingly enough it was. And he produced a document to prove it. Winston Harry Churchill, an absolutely splendid person.

To speed up the process of recovery in these and other places, we have a whole battery of special measures and programmes – you heard about them from Kenneth Clarke [then the Minister responsible for co-ordinating the Government's inner-city policies]: special measures and programmes to clear derelict land, to renovate run-down council estates, to regenerate city centres, and to turn dereliction into development. But by themselves these measures are not enough. We must also give people in the inner cities the opportunity to improve their own lives and the belief that they can do it. The major reforms in our programme are of course designed for the whole country. But they will be of particular benefit to inner cities.

We will free tenants from their dependence on council landlords. We will free parents to choose the schools they want for their children. We will free businesses in the urban development areas from irksome planning restrictions and controls. And with our rate reform legislation, Socialist councils will no longer be able to drive out small businesses and destroy employment by imposing sky-high rates. Above all, the community charge will make local councils far more accountable to all their voters.

Taken together, these measures will greatly reduce the power of the local council over tenants, parents, pupils and businesses; and greatly increase the opportunities open to those very people. To coin a phrase it is an 'irreversible shift . . . of power . . . in favour of working people and their families.'*

The social problems of some inner cities are deep-seated. Quick and easy solutions are not possible. But the philosophy of enterprise and opportunity, which has put the spark back into our national economy is the way – and the only way – to rejuvenate our cities and restore their confidence and pride.

But our greatest concern, in inner cities and elsewhere, is to reverse the tide of crime for it disfigures all our lives. On Wednesday, we debated crime with a depth of concern that reflects the feelings of every decent person in the country.

Crime invades homes; it breaks hearts; it drags down neighbourhoods; and it spreads fear. The Government is playing its full part in the fight against crime. We have strengthened the police. We have introduced tougher sentences. Violent crime concerns us, above all. It's not just that violent crime is worse than other crime. It's much worse. And that's why we are now taking still tougher action against knives and against guns.

Even so the feeling persists that some of the sentences passed by the courts have not measured up to the enormity of crime. And so as Douglas Hurd announced this week, we shall be introducing legislation to provide for an appeal against sentences which are too lenient. May I point out it will be the second time this Government has brought a measure of this kind before Parliament. I hope that this time it will receive a speedy passage on to the statute book.

But we shall make little progress in the drive against crime if we expect the police and the courts to take on the whole burden. When we are sick, we turn to the doctor; yet we accept responsibility for taking care of our health. When fire breaks out, we call in the Fire Brigade; yet we know it is up to us to take sensible precautions against fire. So it is with crime. There is enormous scope for the public to help the police in what, after all, is a common duty: in neighbourhood watch; in business watch; in crime prevention; in prompt reporting of crime seen or suspected; and in readiness to give evidence.

But even that is not enough. Civilised society doesn't just happen. It has to be sustained by standards widely accepted and upheld.

We must draw on the moral energy of society. And we must draw on the values of family life. For the family is where first we learn those habits of mutual love, tolerance and service on which every healthy nation depends for its survival. It was Sir William Haley, the great editor of *The Times*, who, twenty years ago, said this, 'There are things which are bad and false and ugly and no amount of argument or

* Labour's General Election Manifesto, October 1974

specious casuistry will make them good or true or beautiful. It is time that these things were said'. And he said them.

But if we are to succeed today, all those in authority must recover that confidence and speak with a strong, emphatic and single voice. Because too often, they speak in different and conflicting voices.

The great majority of crimes are committed by young people, in their teens and early twenties. It is on such impressionable young people that anti-police propaganda and the glamourisation of crime can have the most deadly effect. When left-wing councils and left-wing teachers criticise the police they give moral sanction to the criminally inclined. When the broadcasters flout their own standards on violent television programmes, they risk a brutalising effect on the morally unstable. When the Labour Party refuses to support the Prevention of Terrorism Act – an Act that saves lives – they weaken society, they weaken society's resistance to the modern scourge of terrorism.

Local councils, teachers, broadcasters, politicians: all of us have a responsibility to uphold the civilised values which underpin the law. We owe it to society of which we are a part. And we owe it especially to future generations who will inherit the society that we create.

Our conference takes place at a time which could prove to be a historic turning point in world affairs. And we can say – with some pride – that Britain has played a major part in creating the opportunities which now open up before us.

It is, of course, a time of tension and even of danger in the Persian Gulf. But there, too, Britain is giving a strong lead. And I do indeed pay tribute to both Geoffrey Howe and you, Mr President [George Younger, the Defence Secretary], for the lead which you have given. May I join you, Mr President, in speaking for this whole conference – and indeed for the people of this country – when I express our thanks and appreciation to the Merchant Officers and seamen who sail that vital waterway; and to the Royal Navy's Armilla Patrol and its minesweepers which protect them. We honour their dedication and their courage.

But today is also a time of hope. Indeed there is no mistaking the bracing air of change in the Soviet Union. In my many hours of talking with Mr Gorbachev in Moscow earlier this year, his determination to bring about far-reaching reform was plain. The difficulties and obstacles confronting him are massive.

But we must recognise that anything which increases human liberty, which extends the boundaries of discussion and which increases initiative and enterprise in the Soviet Union, is of fundamental importance in terms of human rights. And that's why we support it. That is why we have publicly welcomed and encouraged those aspects of Mr Gorbachev's reforms which do just this. They are genuinely courageous – not least in their admission that, after seventy years, the socialist system has failed to produce the standard of life the Russian people want.

But we have yet to see that change carried through into the Soviet Union's policies towards the outside world. The traditional instruments of Soviet power – military strength, subversion, propaganda – are all being exercised as vigorously as ever. Afghanistan is still occupied. The Berlin Wall still stands, and Soviet weapons are still pouring into Third World countries which need food but not arms. They get the food from the free world and arms from the Soviet Union.

There is, however, hope in the agreement which now seems certain to be signed later this autumn, by the United States and the Soviet Union, to eliminate medium and shorter-range nuclear missiles. We welcome that agreement. Indeed Britain has contributed in a major way to its achievement. It's a success for the West – especially for the United States and President Reagan.

But let us remember one thing. If we had listened to the Labour Party and to CND – insofar as you can distinguish between the two – that agreement would never have been achieved. The Russians would have kept their thirteen hundred nuclear warheads, while the West would have given away its three hundred, for nothing in return. That lesson must never be forgotten. Reductions in nuclear weapons come about not from weakness, but from strength.

Our policies, Conservative policies, are bearing fruit and we have every reason to be pleased. But we must not let satisfaction turn to euphoria.

We are ready for improved relations with the Soviet Union. But we can't afford to take anything on trust. Nor should we be deceived by changes in style rather than substance. We shall continue to judge the Soviet Union not by what they say but by what they do.

We believe that the strategic nuclear weapons of the United States and the Soviet Union could be reduced by 50 per cent without endangering western security. But so long as the Soviet Union continues to enjoy massive superiority in chemical and conventional forces, we say that reductions in nuclear weapons in Europe have gone far enough. As the Supreme Allied Commander in Europe reminded us recently: it is not a nuclear-free Europe we want, it is a war-free Europe. Nuclear weapons will continue to play a vital role in preventing war in Europe – as they have done for forty years. And that is why we will press ahead with Trident and the modernisation of our independent deterrent, vital to our security.

The British people want peace. But it must be a peace with freedom and justice. And that peace is only maintained by keeping our defence strong, by resisting violence and intimidation at home, and by standing up to tyrants and terrorists abroad. That is the true spirit of the British people. That is the spirit which sustained us through two world wars. And it guides us still.

You may perhaps have heard that I'm a faithful student of Rudyard Kipling. Occasionally, I've even been known to quote him. So it won't come as a complete surprise if I refer to his poem 'Recessional', in which he warned us to beware of boasting and to keep 'A humble and a contrite heart'. That's sound advice to any Government.

But may I say today we have both a right and a duty to remind the whole free world that, once more, Britain is confident, strong, trusted. Confident, because attitudes have changed. 'Can't be done' has given way to 'What's to stop us?' Strong, because our economy is enterprising, competitive and expanding. And trusted, because we are known to be a powerful ally and a faithful friend. All this has been made possible by the national revival which we have carried through. And everyone in this hall, and millions outside it, can claim a share in that revival.

Now, once again, it has fallen to the Conservatives to lead the nation into the 1990s. Let us face that future with quiet confidence born of what we have accomplished in the last eight years.

Britain's institutions are shaped by the character of her people. It's all that is gifted, just and fair in that character which reassures our friends and allies; and brings hope to those who have yet to know the liberty we take for granted.

It is a great trust which has been placed in our care. May we never fail that trust.

14

> CONSERVATIVE
> PARTY CONFERENCE
>
> * BRIGHTON *
>
> 14th October 1988

FOUR YEARS HAVE PASSED since we last came to Brighton for our conference. We all have memories of that week: memories sad and memories brave. But the human spirit is indomitable. Today we take inspiration from those of our friends, many of them here in this hall, friends who survived to rededicate themselves to the cause of freedom.

All elections matter. But some matter more than others. Some elections are not just part of history. They make history. And such was our Conservative victory in 1979. After a series of Socialist Governments that said 'we can't', Britain wanted a Government that said 'we can'. And it got one.

Nearly ten years in government – how much energy and commitment we have all put into the battle. And no one more so than the great friend and colleague we are delighted to have with us today – Willie Whitelaw. Nearly ten years in Government – and a resurgence of freedom and prosperity without parallel. Nearly ten years – yet it's still we Conservatives who set the pace, generate the ideas, and have the vision.

Alone among the political parties, we hold fast to our convictions. But next year's tenth anniversary is no time to rest on our laurels. It marks the start of our next ten. We are all too young to put our feet up.

I'm not so sure though about our political opponents. They don't seem to have had too good a summer. After the two platoons of the old Alliance went their separate ways, they popped up last month at Torquay and Blackpool respectively. The second called the first one names, but seemed to have some difficulty knowing what name to call themselves. All those initials are so confusing, aren't they? I suggested SOS – but clearly things have gone too far for that. In the end, I think they decided to be one thing in the country and whatever they felt like in the House of Commons. Or was it the other way round?

As for Labour's goings on at Blackpool, for half an hour or so it seemed that their leader had seen the light and would shortly be calling his memoirs 'I did it her way'. Whatever happened to

Socialism? I began to compose a gracious little tribute to get the new session off to a bright start. Alas, for high hopes. Was Labour about to shake off its union shackles and go it alone? Not on your Todd, – and that is positively the last Todd joke at this conference.

So it's back to square one for the Socialists. The Labour leopard can't change its spots – even if it sometimes thinks wistfully of a blue rinse.

Nearly ten years into this Conservative Government and everybody knows that our policies work and that Labour's don't; and that our policies have produced a standard of living undreamed of by our parents and the highest standard of social services this country has ever known.

The Japanese call it Britain's economic miracle – and who are we to argue? I'm proud that with a Conservative Government people are better off than they've ever been before. But an odd thing has happened recently. Because we strive to increase the prosperity of the nation and its citizens, we're accused of materialism. It's a curious charge. For years one of the main arguments in British politics was how to secure economic growth. Now we've done that, now we've halted and reversed the years of decline over which Labour presided, we are told that all we care about is 'loadsamoney'.

Because we give people the chance to better themselves, they accuse us of encouraging selfishness and greed. What nonsense. Does someone's natural desire to do well for himself, to build a better life for his family and provide opportunities for his children, does all this make him a materialist? Of course it doesn't. It makes him a decent human being, committed to his family and his community, *and* prepared to take responsibility on his own shoulders.

The truth is that what we are actually encouraging is the best in human nature. The prosperity brought about by our policies offers a wider choice to more people than ever before. Yes, our children can travel to see the treasures and wonders of the world. Yes, older people can enjoy greater comfort and pursue their own interest. Yes, culture and the arts are thriving. Yes, people can expect to enjoy these things. If that is the charge, Madam President, I plead guilty.

There's another reply to Labour's charge of materialism. Our approach has meant more to spend on the social services; more on the Health Service; and more on the disabled. Indeed, if you measure community concern by community spending – as Labour does – we win hands down every time.

Now, of course, we don't expect the Labour Party to have anything good to say about us. After all, they have hardly anything good to say about each other. But it's time we took the credit for some of the things we have achieved. For example: eight million patients are treated in hospitals each year; an 80 per cent increase has taken place in spending on benefits for the disabled; and there has been an increase in *real* terms of *45 per cent* in nurses' pay. It's not for Labour who cut nurses' pay, and cut hospital building, to lecture Conservatives on care and compassion.

Our Government has made enormous increases in the amount spent on social welfare to help the less fortunate – and so have individuals. As prosperity has increased, so the fundamental generosity of our people has prompted far more personal giving. Of course, there will always be a minority whose sole concern is themselves. But those who care, and they are the great majority of us, now have the means to give. And they are giving in full measure: over £1,500 million a year to boost charities, rebuild churches, help medical research and feed the hungry. That's a marvellous record. And it doesn't stop at individuals. Many businesses are now giving a percentage of their profits to help the community in which they are situated.

Is this materialism? Is this the selfish society? Are these the hallmarks of greed? The fact is that prosperity has created not the selfish society but the generous society. Labour's charge is absurd.

So our critics come up with a new charge. They say the individual gains success only at the expense of the community. That's wrong, too. Personal effort doesn't undermine the community; it enhances the community. When individual talents are held back, the community is held back too. Encourage the individual and the community benefits. A parent's success is shared by his family, a pupil's success by his school, a soldier's by his regiment. A man may climb Everest for himself, but at the summit he plants his country's flag.

We can only build a responsible, independent community with responsible, independent people. That's why Conservative policies have given more and more of them the chance to buy their own homes, to build up capital, to acquire shares in their companies.

But there are some people – such as those living on housing estates controlled by hard-Left councils or parents with children going to inadequate schools – who, by the time of the last election, had not benefited from our policies as much as we'd like. Our last manifesto had those people especially in mind.

That's why we're giving council tenants new rights in housing. We believe that where families have a bigger say in their own home, the whole street looks up. In some areas, it's already happening. And we're giving parents more say in their children's education. We believe that if parents help to run schools, we'll get the best schools not just for their children, but for all children.

But it's not enough to pass new laws at Westminster. We have to see that the benefits reach the people for whom they were intended. And we have to do that. We have to help those families. Otherwise they'll be browbeaten by Socialist councillors and bombarded by

Socialist propaganda calculated to deny them the opportunities we have provided.

Greater responsibility gives more dignity to the individual and more strength to the community. That belief is at the heart of Conservatism – and we must make it live.

When we were returned at that historic election in 1979 we were faced with the overriding threat of inflation. It was inflation that had redistributed wealth from the thrifty to the fly-by-night. It was inflation that had undermined confidence, first in the currency, then in savings, then in investment, and finally in our country's future. To salvage our economy, we had first to defeat inflation and only then could the great revival of the British economy begin.

Today we are in our eighth year of growth. Our unemployment figures are below the Community average. We have created more jobs than they have. And other countries come to our shores to see what we do and go home to copy.

Since we took office we have handed eighteen State enterprises back to the British people – eighteen, so far, more to come. We have encouraged ownership at home and ownership at work. We have turned small business from an endangered species into a vital and rapidly growing part of our economy. The habits of hard work, enterprise, and inventiveness that made us great are with us again.

But however firmly rooted our new-found strength, you can't steer an economy on automatic pilot. Success doesn't look after itself. You have to work at it. In economics, there are no final victories.

At home, the fast pace of economic growth has put more money into people's pockets and more money into industry's profits. Some has been invested, but with rapid growth in consumption, imports have grown faster than exports, leaving us with a substantial trade deficit. And too much buying has been paid for by too much borrowing. So to encourage people to spend less and save more, the Chancellor has had to raise interest rates. It's never popular to push them up – except perhaps with savers – but popular or not, the Chancellor has done the right thing, as you'd expect of him. And the right thing is to make sure that we continue to grow steadily, if less fast than in recent months.

Too much borrowing has also meant that inflation today is too high. Make no mistake. We intend to bring inflation down again. That's not an expression of hope. It's a statement of intent. And I think the country knows us well enough by now to recognise that we say what we mean and we mean what we say.

As you know there are always pressures on Government to spend more than the country can afford. We're not going down that road – not this year, not next year, not any year. We'll continue to keep a firm grip on public spending. I look forward to those who so roundly condemn extravagance with private money, giving their whole-hearted enthusiastic support to our prudence in handling the public's money.

There is nothing new or unusual about the Tory commitment to protect the environment. The last thing we want is to leave environmental debts for our children to clear up – slag, grime, acid rain and pollution. For too much of human history, man assumed that whatever he did, he could take his natural world for granted. Today we know that simply isn't true.

In the last century or so, we have seen an unprecedented increase in the pace of change marked by the growth in population, the spread of industry, the dramatically increased use of oil, gas and coal, and the cutting down of forests. These have created new and daunting problems: acid rain and the 'greenhouse effect', a kind of global heat trap and its consequences for the world's climate.

In the past, science has solved many of the problems which at the time seemed quite insuperable. It can do so again. We are far too sensible to think that in 1988 we can turn the clock back to a pre-industrial world where Adam delved and Eve span. The Garden of Eden had a population of two. Our world has a population of five billion going on six. It has more than doubled in my own lifetime. Those people need to cook meals, heat homes, clothe themselves, find work. They need factories, roads, and power stations.

All these things are part of our lives today and the ambition of the third world tomorrow. So the choice facing us is not industrial development or a clean environment. To survive we need both. Industry is part of our habitat; economic growth is one of the systems that sustain human life today.

Pride in these islands – our countryside, our seas and rivers – runs like a thread through our history and literature. Sometimes, it seems a perverse pride. 'Fog, fog everywhere' begins one of Dickens' greatest novels. That was still true in London when I first went to work there. But the Clean Air Act of 1956 – passed by a Conservative Government – banished smog from the air we breathe. The Thames is now the cleanest metropolitan estuary in the world and £4 billion is now being spent on the Mersey. I want to see the industrial rivers of the North and Midlands – and of Europe – as clean as the Thames.

We have led Europe in banning the dumping of harmful industrial waste in the North Sea. And, given our record, we are well placed to take the lead with other governments in practical efforts to protect the wider world. We will work with them to end the destruction of the world's forests. We shall direct more of our overseas aid to help poor countries to protect their trees and plant new ones. We will join with others to seek further protection of the ozone layer – that global skin which protects life itself from ultra-violet radiation. We will work to cut down the use of fossil fuels, a cause of both acid rain and the greenhouse effect. But that means a policy for safe, sensible and balanced use of nuclear power.

It's we Conservatives who are not merely friends of the Earth – we are its guardians and trustees for generations to come. The core of Tory philosophy and the case for protecting the environment are the same. No generation has a freehold on this earth. All we have is a life tenancy – with a full repairing lease. And this Government intends to meet the terms of that lease in full.

Year in, year out, this Conservative Government has taken action against crime – action on police numbers, on police powers, on firearms, on fraud, on prison building, on compensation for victims, on stiffer penalties – and action against football hooligans and those who carry knives and firearms. And there is more to come. Witness, for example, the new Criminal Justice Act.

I hope that the Courts will continue to take account of the strong public support for tough penalties against violent criminals. I am sure they will pay the most careful attention to the longer sentences that are now available to them. Anyone who mugs an old lady leaving the post office with her pension, anyone who rapes a teenager walking home from an evening with friends, anyone who commits violence against a child should have no shred of doubt about the severity of the sentence for that sort of brutality.

Violent crime is a blight on too many lives. And its reduction has a claim not only on the political energy of the Government, but on the moral energy of the people. We are not spectators in the battle between the police and criminals. We are all involved. To witness a crime and say nothing about it, hinders the police and helps the criminal. To protect our own home from burglary hinders the criminal and helps the police.

There's a breed of left-wing politicians who excuse violence on the grounds that it's not the criminal who is guilty – but the rest of us. That's a specious argument left over from the sixties. In effect it excuses, indeed even encourages, crime by absolving the criminal of guilt in advance. Weasel words can never justify the actions of the robber, the thug or the hooligan.

Conservatives need no sermons from Socialists on the rule of law. We proposed tougher sentences for criminals who carry guns: they opposed them. We proposed that over-lenient sentences should be referred to the appeal court: Labour voted against. We condemned violence on the picket line: they equivocated. And, year after year, they will not support the Prevention of Terrorism Act – an act which is vital to the defeat of the IRA and which has saved so very many lives. I find that very hard to forgive.

In this country and in other democracies, the enemies of civilisation and freedom have turned to the gun and the bomb to destroy those they can't persuade. The terrorist threat to freedom is world-wide. It can never be met by appeasement. Give in to the terrorist and you breed more terrorism. At home and abroad our message is the same. We will not bargain, nor compromise, nor bend the knee to terrorists.

In our United Kingdom, the main terrorist threat has come from the IRA. Their minds twisted by hatred and fanaticism, they have tried to bomb and murder their way to their objective of tearing more than a million citizens out of the United Kingdom. The truth is that the whole IRA campaign is based on crushing democracy and smashing anyone who doesn't agree with them.

To all those who have suffered so much at their hands – to the Northern Ireland policemen, prison officers and their families, to the soldiers, the judges, the civil servants and their families – we offer our deepest admiration and thanks for defending democracy and our thanks for facing danger while keeping within the rule of law – unlike the terrorist who skulks in the shadows and shoots to kill.

We thank too the security forces who had the guts to go to Gibraltar to give evidence to the inquest, demonstrating conclusively that they acted at all times within the law and to save lives – the lives of countless people who would have been killed had the IRA fulfilled their murderous purpose. What a pity it is that there are still some in this country not prepared to accept the verdict of the jury, so great is their prejudice against the security forces. What comfort that must be to the terrorists.

We will work to increase co-operation in security between the sovereign governments in London and Dublin. We will work to involve both Protestants and Catholics fully and fairly in the economic and political life of Northern Ireland. But we will never give up the search for more effective ways of defeating the IRA.

If the IRA think they can weary us or frighten us, they have made a terrible miscalculation. People sometimes say that it's wrong to use the word never in politics. I disagree. Some things are of such fundamental importance that no other word is appropriate. So I say again today that this Government will *never* surrender to the IRA. *Never*.

Great changes are taking place in world affairs, no less momentous, no less decisive for our future than those which followed the Second World War. But there is a crucial difference. This time liberty is gaining ground the world over. Communism is in retreat. Democracy and free enterprise are showing that only they can meet the real needs of people.

Britain's resurgence and our close relationship with the United States under President Reagan's strong leadership has put us right at the forefront of these great events. And once again we are playing the part which history and our instincts demand.

President Reagan has rebuilt the strength and confidence of the West – not without a little help – and he has inspired the democracies to go out and win the battle of ideas. It's vital that Britain and America should always stand together. So the next President of the United States will have the United Kingdom as a staunch ally. The need for strong leadership in America and in Britain will be no less in the period ahead.

Perhaps one day the exciting developments taking place in the Soviet Union will lead to a freer society and less expansionist aims. Let us hope so. But hope is no basis for a defence policy. For all the bold reforms, the Soviet Union remains a one-party state, in which the Communist Party is supreme, and Soviet forces remain far in excess of what they need for defence alone. So we have to keep our sense of perspective and our defences in good repair. The old dangers persist and we also have to be alert to new dangers. Even as relations with the Soviet Union become more hopeful, some other countries have already acquired chemical weapons and missiles. And what's more, some seek nuclear weapons.

It's in the nature of democracies to relax at the first sign of hope. *This we must not do.* For great change is also a time of great uncertainty, especially in the countries of Eastern Europe. Now more than ever before the West must be united and prepared.

NATO's purpose is to prevent not only nuclear war but all war. And its strategy recognises that conventional weapons alone can't provide an adequate and effective deterrent against either nuclear threat or the massive conventional and chemical weapons of the Warsaw Pact.

Yet, last week in Blackpool, Labour reduced the defence of the realm to a farce. Their new secret weapon for Britain's defence was revealed. It was a form of words. Labour's leadership proposed a composite resolution embracing unilateral disarmament, bilateral disarmament and multilateral disarmament, all at the same time. Not to defend Britain against her enemies, but to defend the Labour leader against his. And like all forms of appeasement it failed.

The Labour conference passed a resolution reaffirming Labour's commitment to one-sided disarmament. But the only resolution that matters is the unswerving resolution of this Conservative Government. The British people know that it is our strength which keeps us safe.

As you know, I spoke recently in Bruges about Britain's views on Europe. It caused a bit of a stir. Indeed, from some of the reactions you would have thought I had re-opened the Hundred Years War. And from the avalanche of support, you'd have thought I'd won it single-handed.

Why all the fuss? Because I reminded people that Europe was not created by the Treaty of Rome? Because I said that willing and active co-operation between *independent sovereign states* is the best way to build a successful European Community? Because I said that to try to suppress nationhood and concentrate power at the centre of a European conglomerate would be highly damaging and would jeopardize the objectives we seek to achieve?

Of course, that wasn't at all convenient for those who want to bring about a federal Europe by stealth. They don't like having these points aired publicly. That was evident from their confusion. First they argued that national identity is *not* threatened by Brussels. Then they said that the whole idea of nationhood is old-fashioned and out-of-date. Well, they can't have it both ways!

But I welcomed the debate, because it's brought into the open an equally fundamental question. The choice between two kinds of Europe: a Europe based on the widest possible freedom for enterprise; or a Europe governed by Socialist methods of centralised control and regulation. There's no doubt what the Community's founders intended. The Treaty of Rome is a charter for economic liberty, which they knew was the essential condition for personal and political liberty.

Today that founding concept is under attack from those who see European unity as a vehicle for spreading Socialism. We haven't worked all these years to free Britain from the paralysis of Socialism only to see it creep in through the back door of central control and bureaucracy from Brussels. That wasn't what we joined the European Community for. *Ours* is the true European ideal. It is that ideal which will fire our campaign in the European elections. That's why we must win every possible seat in the European Parliament for the Conservative cause.

We shall point out that Britain has taken the lead in tackling practical issues in Europe which are of real benefit to people – reform of the Common Agricultural Policy, completion of the Single Market, the fight against terrorism and drugs; that Britain continues to make the second largest financial contribution to Europe; and that Britain stations more forces beyond its borders – nearly 70,000 of them – than any other European country in defence of freedom. With these sorts of credentials no one should doubt Britain's wholehearted commitment to Europe.

Every year the press tells us in advance that Conservative conferences are dull affairs in which everyone agrees with everyone else. And every year we have a debate on law and order. Still, the press is right in one respect. Everyone can see, through all the cut-and-thrust of debate, that this Party is united on the great fundamentals of politics.

We believe that individuals have a right to liberty that no state can take away; that Government is the servant of the people, not its master; that the role of Government is to *strengthen* our freedom, not deny it; that the economic role of Government is to establish a climate in which enterprise can flourish, not to elbow enterprise out of the way; that a wise Government will spread opportunities, but that individuals must seize them; that citizens who are protected by the law have a duty to assist in maintaining the law; that freedom entails responsibilities, first to the family, then to neighbours, then to the nation – and beyond; and that a strong Britain is the surest guarantor of peace. As well as these grand themes, we have always believed in what is small and precious, in the value of what is local and familiar, in the patchworks of voluntary groups and associations, each with its own purpose, but all pursuing the common purpose of making the country a better and more civilised place.

These are the beliefs which sustain us. Other parties may discard their principles along with their names or seek to conceal their beliefs in order to win power. We hold by the principles we know to be right – not right because they serve our interests; not even right just because they work; but right because they express all that is best in human nature. Nothing less would have sustained us through the difficult early days of this Government; nothing less would have ensured the loyalty of our supporters and the trust of the British people when the going wasn't so good. But we had – and we have – the great assurance that our beliefs are not lofty abstractions confined to philosophy lectures. They are the common sense of the British people. They are what ordinary men and women agree on instinctively.

The Conservative Party occupies the common ground of British politics. Indeed, we staked out that ground. And it is where the great mass of the British people have pitched their tents. So it has fallen to us to lead Britain into the 1990s. And, who knows, beyond.

There will be new challenges, new problems, new tests. For there are no final victories in politics either. But we will meet them strengthened by our belief in this country; in the talents and wisdom of its people; in their tolerance and fairness; in their decency and kindness; and in their confidence and their courage.